DAY HIKES AROUND
SANTA
BARBARA

82 GREAT HIKES

by Robert Stone

Day Hike Books, Inc.
RED LODGE, MONTANA

Published by Day Hike Books, Inc.
P.O. Box 865
Red Lodge, Montana 59068

Distributed by The Globe Pequot Press
246 Goose Lane
P.O. Box 480
Guilford, CT 06437-0480
800-243-0495 (direct order) · 800-820-2329 (fax order)
www.globe-pequot.com

Photographs by Robert Stone
Design by Paula Doherty

The author has made every attempt to provide accurate information in this book. However, trail routes and features may change—please use common sense and forethought, and be mindful of your own capabilities. Let this book guide you, but be aware that each hiker assumes responsibility for their own safety. The author and publisher do not assume any responsibility for loss, damage or injury caused through the use of this book.

Cover photo:
Mission Creek and Little Fern Canyon Falls—Hikes 37, 38 and 39
Back cover photo: Refugio State Beach—Hike 72

Table of Contents

Montecito

Santa Barbara

Goleta

East Camino Cielo Road · Santa Ynez River Valley

Upper Santa Ynez Area

Lower Santa Ynez Area—Paradise Road

Lake Cachuma Area

North Country
Santa Maria • Lompoc • Buellton • Solvang

About the Hikes
and the Santa Barbara area

Santa Barbara is a captivating, inviting community that is located in a beautiful, natural setting along the Pacific coast. The temperate climate and refreshing ocean breezes, very similar to the Mediterranean, have distinguished this area as "the jewel of the American Riviera."

Santa Barbara lies in a unique area. The landscape around the city includes mountainous terrain, preserved forests and wilderness areas, and stretches of undeveloped coast. To the north of the coast, the Santa Ynez Mountains rise 3,000 feet, serving as a backdrop to Santa Barbara and the nearby coastal communities. These mountains separate the coastal plain from the rolling farmlands and mountainous interior of Santa Barbara County. The incredible Big Sur coastline lies farther up the coast between Santa Barbara and Monterey. The cities of San Luis Obispo (100 miles northwest) and Los Angeles (90 miles south) are a comfortable drive away.

Day Hikes Around Santa Barbara is a comprehensive guide to 82 day hikes within a 50-mile radius of the city. The trails have been chosen for their scenery, variety and ability to be hiked within a day. The network of hiking trails around Santa Barbara stretches along the coast, up and over the Santa Ynez Mountains, and throughout the Santa Ynez River Valley. These hikes include an excellent cross section of scenery and difficulty level, ranging from coastal beach walks to steep canyon climbs with far reaching views. Highlights include oceanside bluffs; beaches; tidepools; wetland preserves; sculpted gorges; rock outcroppings with caves; numerous waterfalls and secluded pools in mossy canyons; mountain ridge trails; historical sites; stunning overlooks of wide mountain valleys, towns and the Pacific Ocean; and some of southern California's best scenery.

Hikes 1—17 are found in the area around the city of Ojai in neighboring Ventura County. Nearly all of the hikes here travel along river valleys and canyons. The lightly used trails wind through national forest and wilderness land.

Farther west lie the coastal communities of Carpinteria, Summerland and Montecito, Hikes 18—33. Coastal hikes include tidepools, beaches and wildlife viewing areas. A short distance inland, trails and abandoned roads crisscross the foothills and canyons that lead down to the ocean.

Hikes 34—51 are found in the immediate vicinity of Santa Barbara, Goleta and Isla Vista. Natural, undeveloped scenery surrounds the majority of the trails. Several hikes lead up through cool river canyons to great coastal and city overlooks. Undeveloped parks and wildlife habitats offer shady retreats just minutes from the urban areas.

The Camino Cielo Road travels along the ridge that divides the coastline from the Santa Ynez River Valley. Hikes 52—67 are found in this area, known as the Upper Country. These 15 backcountry hikes are found from the ridge to the valley below. Some of the hikes follow the Santa Ynez River Valley and its tributaries. Several others are high elevation climbs that offer the reward of 360-degree panoramic views.

The North Country, Hikes 68—82, stretches from Lake Cachuma to the northern county line along the Santa Maria River. Here you will find mountainous backcountry, coastal bluffs, secluded beaches, a historic mission and the highest sand dunes on the west coast.

All of these hikes are found within an hour's drive of Santa Barbara and can be completed within a day. (Map sources and references are included for extending the hikes.) An overall map of the hikes is found on the next page. There are four additional area maps with further detail, also noted on the overall map. Each of the hikes is accompanied with a map, detailed driving and hiking directions, and a quick overview of distance/time/elevation. Use this information and the hike summaries to choose a trail appropriate to your ability and desire.

A few basic necessities will make your hike more enjoyable. Wear supportive, comfortable hiking shoes. Bring hats, sunscreen, sunglasses, drinking water, snacks and appropriate outerwear. Bring swimwear and outdoor gear if heading to the beaches. Ticks may be prolific and poison oak flourishes in the canyons and shady moist areas. Exercise caution by using insect repellent and staying on the trails.

Hiking around Santa Barbara will give you a new appreciation of the beauty of this region. Enjoy your day hike as you discover southern California out on the trails!

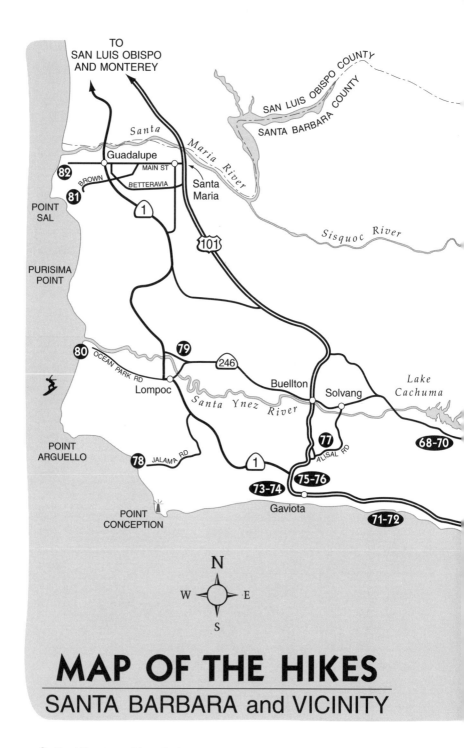

MAP OF THE HIKES
SANTA BARBARA and VICINITY

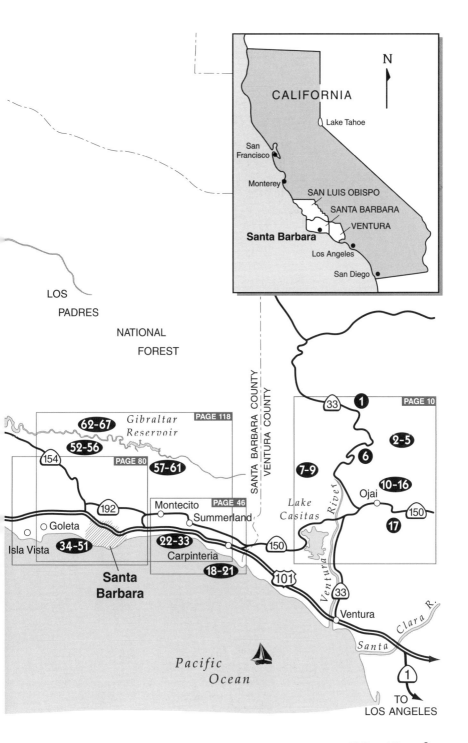

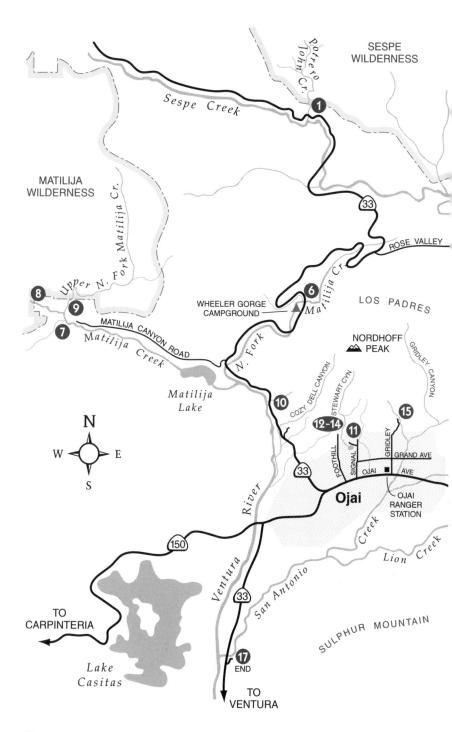

SESPE
WILDERNESS

MATILIJA
WILDERNESS

Sespe Creek

Potrero John Cr.

33

ROSE VALLEY

LOS PADRES

Upper N. Fork Matilija Cr.

N. Fork Matilija Cr.

WHEELER GORGE
CAMPGROUND

Matilija Cr.

NORDHOFF
PEAK

GRIDLEY CANYON

8

9

7

MATILIJA CANYON ROAD

Matilija Creek

Matilija
Lake

N. Fork

COZY DELL CANYON

STEWART CYN

6

10

12–14

11

15

FOOTHILL

SIGNAL

GRIDLEY

GRAND AVE

N
W — E
S

33

OJAI AVE

Ojai

OJAI
RANGER
STATION

150

Ventura River

San Antonio Creek

Lion Creek

TO
CARPINTERIA

Lake
Casitas

33

17
END

SULPHUR MOUNTAIN

TO
VENTURA

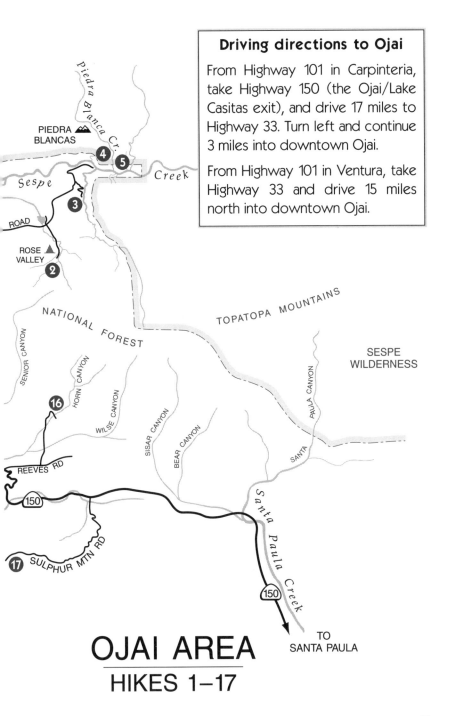

Driving directions to Ojai

From Highway 101 in Carpinteria, take Highway 150 (the Ojai/Lake Casitas exit), and drive 17 miles to Highway 33. Turn left and continue 3 miles into downtown Ojai.

From Highway 101 in Ventura, take Highway 33 and drive 15 miles north into downtown Ojai.

PIEDRA BLANCAS

Piedra Blanca Cr.

Sespe Creek

ROAD

ROSE VALLEY

NATIONAL FOREST

TOPATOPA MOUNTAINS

SESPE WILDERNESS

SENIOR CANYON

HORN CANYON

WILSE CANYON

SISAR CANYON

BEAR CANYON

PAULA CANYON

SANTA

REEVES RD

150

SULPHUR MTN RD

Santa Paula Creek

150

TO SANTA PAULA

OJAI AREA
HIKES 1–17

Hike 1
Potrero John Trail

Hiking distance: 4 miles round trip
Hiking time: 2 hours
Elevation gain: 600 feet
Maps: U.S.G.S. Wheeler Springs
        Sespe Wilderness Trail Map

Summary of hike: The Potrero John Trail is an uncrowded, lightly used trail in the 220,000-acre Sespe Wilderness, part of Los Padres National Forest. The hike begins at an elevation of 3,655 feet, where Potrero John Creek empties into Sespe Creek. The trail follows Potrero John Creek through a narrow gorge and up the canyon. There is also an open meadow dotted with red baked manzanita and views of the surrounding mountains. At the trail's end is Potrero John Camp, a creekside flat shaded with oaks.

Driving directions: From Ojai, drive 21 miles north on Highway 33 (Maricopa Highway) to the trailhead parking pullout on the right side of the road. It is located on the north side of Potrero Bridge.

Hiking directions: Hike north past the trailhead sign, immediately entering the narrow, steep-walled canyon on the west side of Potrero John Creek. After three successive creek crossings, the trail enters the Sespe Wilderness. There are eight creek crossings in the first mile while passing various pools and cascades. At one mile, the trail leaves the narrow canyon, emerging into a large, open meadow. At the far side of the meadow, the trail ends at Potrero John Camp, a walk-in camp on the banks of the creek. To return, retrace your steps.

To hike further, a rough, unmaintained trail heads upstream over rocks, underbrush and downfall. Along the way there are continuous pools, cascades and small waterfalls.

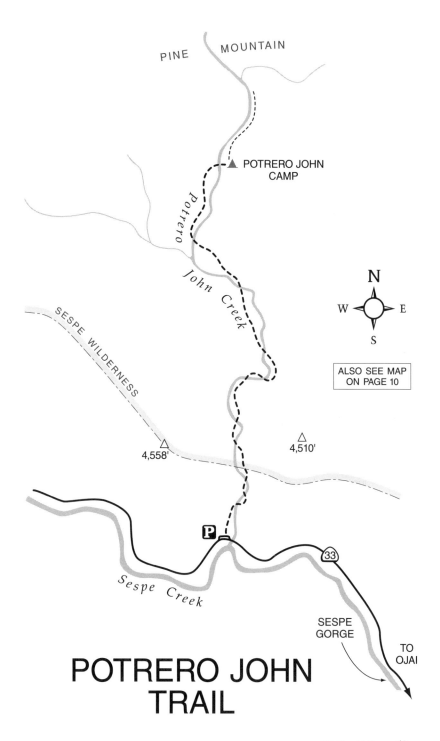

PINE MOUNTAIN

▲ POTRERO JOHN CAMP

Potrero

John Creek

SESPE WILDERNESS

N
W ◆ E
S

ALSO SEE MAP
ON PAGE 10

△ 4,558'

△ 4,510'

P

33

Sespe Creek

SESPE
GORGE

TO
OJAI

POTRERO JOHN TRAIL

Hike 2
Rose Valley Falls

Hiking distance: 0.8 miles round trip
Hiking time: 30 minutes
Elevation gain: 300 feet
Maps: U.S.G.S. Lion Canyon
Sespe Wilderness Trail Map

Summary of hike: Rose Valley Falls is a 300-foot, two-tiered waterfall. This hike follows Rose Valley Creek up a shady canyon to the base of the lower falls, a 100-foot, multi-strand waterfall. The waterfall cascades over the sheer sandstone cliffs onto the rocks below in a cool, moss covered grotto. This short, easy trail begins at the Rose Valley Campground at an elevation of 3,450 feet. There are also three lakes near the campground that are stocked with trout.

Driving directions: From Ojai, drive 14.6 miles north on Highway 33 (Maricopa Highway) to the Rose Valley turnoff and turn right. Continue 3 miles to the Rose Valley Campground turnoff across from the lower lake and turn right. Drive 0.6 miles to the south end of the campground loop road to the signed trailhead by campsite number 4.

Hiking directions: Hike south past the trailhead sign, immediately entering the thick oak, bay and sycamore forest on the well-defined trail. Cross the creek and stay on the main path as you make your way up the lush, narrow canyon. The first of several small waterfalls can be spotted on the left at 0.2 miles. Short side paths lead down to the creek by these waterfalls and pools. The trail ends in less than a half mile at the base of lower Rose Valley Falls with its bridal veil beauty. Return along the same path.

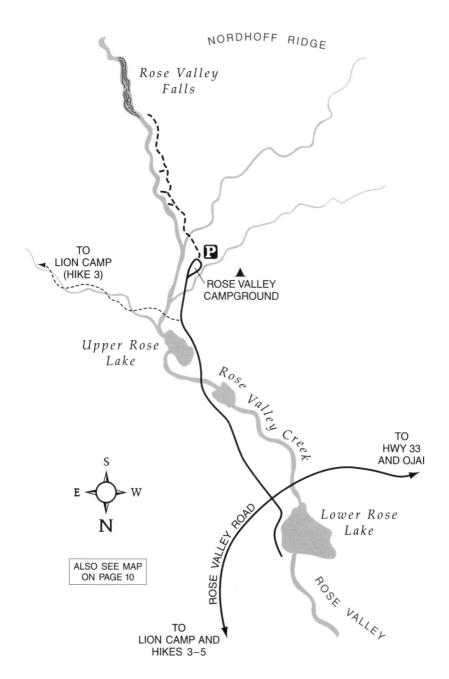

NORDHOFF RIDGE

Rose Valley Falls

TO
LION CAMP
(HIKE 3)

P

ROSE VALLEY
CAMPGROUND

Upper Rose Lake

Rose Valley Creek

TO
HWY 33
AND OJAI

S

E ⟡ W

N

Lower Rose Lake

ROSE VALLEY ROAD

ALSO SEE MAP
ON PAGE 10

ROSE VALLEY

TO
LION CAMP AND
HIKES 3–5

ROSE VALLEY FALLS

Hike 3
Lion Canyon Trail
to West Fork Lion Camp

Hiking distance: 5 miles round trip
Hiking time: 2.5 hours
Elevation gain: 350 feet
Maps: U.S.G.S. Lion Canyon
          Sespe Wilderness Trail Map

Summary of hike: The West Fork Lion Camp sits along the banks of the creek on a shady flat. Minutes beyond the camp is a beautiful waterfall and deep pool surrounded by rocks. The trail to the camp heads up the forested Lion Canyon parallel to Lion Canyon Creek.

Driving directions: From Ojai, drive 14.6 miles north on Highway 33 (Maricopa Highway) to the Rose Valley turnoff and turn right. Continue 4.8 miles to a road split. Take the right fork 0.8 miles down to the Middle Lion Campground and trailhead parking area.

Hiking directions: Walk east along the unpaved campground road, crossing Lion Canyon Creek. Take the signed trail to the right, and head south up Lion Canyon. Continue hiking gradually uphill along the east side of the canyon. At 1.3 miles is a posted junction with the Rose-Lion Connector Trail to the right (Hike 2). Proceed straight ahead, staying in Lion Canyon, to another creek crossing at two miles. After crossing is a three-way trail split known as Four Points Trail Junction. To the left, 0.5 miles ahead, is East Fork Lion Camp and a waterfall that lies within the Sespe Wilderness. Straight ahead is the steep trail up to Nordhoff Ridge. Take the right fork and stay on the east side of the creek along the edge of the rocky hillside. Less than a half mile from the junction is the West Fork Lion Camp. Rock hop up the narrow drainage a short distance past the camp to a beautiful waterfall and pool. Return by retracing your steps.

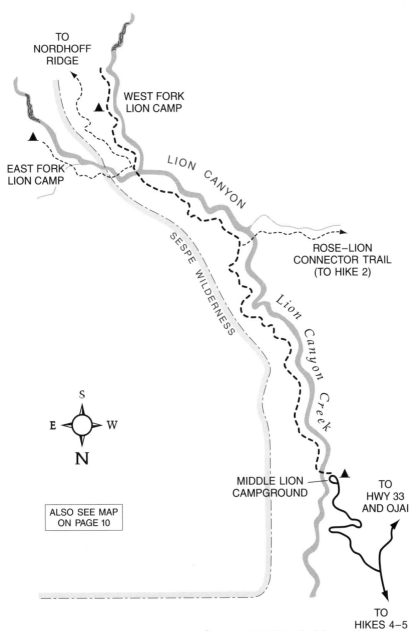

TO
NORDHOFF
RIDGE

WEST FORK
LION CAMP

EAST FORK
LION CAMP

LION CANYON

ROSE–LION
CONNECTOR TRAIL
(TO HIKE 2)

SESPE WILDERNESS

Lion Canyon Creek

S

E ✦ W

N

MIDDLE LION
CAMPGROUND

TO
HWY 33
AND OJAI

ALSO SEE MAP
ON PAGE 10

TO
HIKES 4–5

LION CANYON TRAIL
TO WEST FORK LION CAMP

Hike 4
Piedra Blanca Formations
GENE MARSHALL—PIEDRA BLANCA NATIONAL RECREATION TRAIL

Hiking distance: 2. 5 miles round trip
Hiking time: 1.5 hours
Elevation gain: 300 feet
Maps: U.S.G.S. Lion Canyon
        Sespe Wilderness Trail Map

Summary of hike: The magnificent Piedra Blanca Formations in the Sespe Wilderness are huge, white rounded sandstone outcroppings sculpted by wind and water. The Gene Marshall–Piedra Blanca National Recreation Trail leads past these massive formations. You can easily spend the day exploring the trails around the unique rocks, cavities and caves.

Driving directions: From Ojai, drive 14.6 miles north on Highway 33 (Maricopa Highway) to the Rose Valley turnoff and turn right. Continue 4.8 miles to a road split. Take the left fork one mile down to the Lion Campground and trailhead parking lot at the road's end along the banks of Sespe Creek.

Hiking directions: Rock hop across wide Sespe Creek. Continue to the trailhead sign and trail junction. The right fork is the Sespe River Trail (Hike 5). Take the left fork, heading north towards Piedra Blanca Camp. The trail crosses through chaparral hills past a creekbed to another junction. The left fork heads west towards Howard Creek and Beaver Campground. Proceed to the right, entering the Sespe Wilderness, towards the prominent Piedra Blanca formations. At the formations, leave the main trail and explore the area, choosing your own route. Return along the main trail back to the trailhead.

To hike further, the trail continues north, descending into a small canyon and across a stream. The trail parallels Piedra Blanca Creek up canyon to Piedra Blanca Camp at 2.4 miles. Twin Forks Camp is a half mile further.

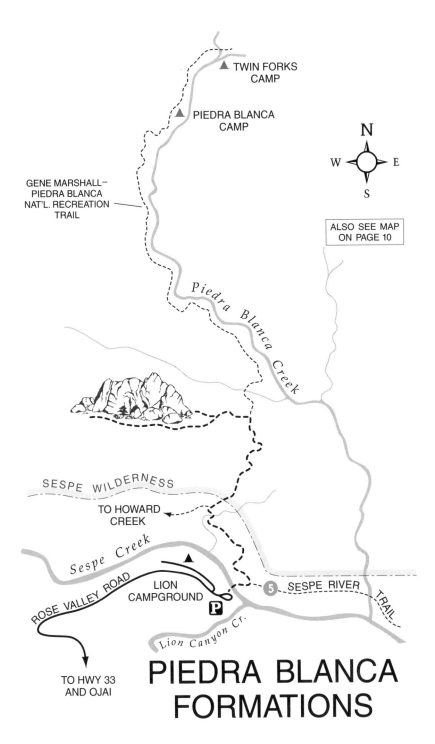

TWIN FORKS
CAMP

PIEDRA BLANCA
CAMP

N
W — E
S

ALSO SEE MAP
ON PAGE 10

GENE MARSHALL–
PIEDRA BLANCA
NAT'L. RECREATION
TRAIL

Piedra Blanca Creek

SESPE WILDERNESS

TO HOWARD
CREEK

Sespe Creek

ROSE VALLEY ROAD

LION
CAMPGROUND
P

5 SESPE RIVER TRAIL

Lion Canyon Cr.

TO HWY 33
AND OJAI

PIEDRA BLANCA
FORMATIONS

Hike 5
Sespe River Trail

Hiking distance: 3.5 miles round trip
Hiking time: 2 hours
Elevation gain: 200 feet
Maps: U.S.G.S. Lion Canyon
 Sespe Wilderness Trail Map

Summary of hike: Sespe Creek is a wide body of water that appears more like a river than a creek. This hike follows a portion of the Old Sespe Road into the Sespe Wilderness to a scenic overlook. The trail parallels the creek past deep pools and sandy flats, crossing Piedra Blanca and Trout Creeks. The 18-mile Old Sespe Road eventually leads to Sespe Hot Springs.

Driving directions: From Ojai, drive 14.6 miles north on Highway 33 (Maricopa Highway) to the Rose Valley turnoff and turn right. Continue 4.8 miles to a road split. Take the left fork one mile down to the Lion Campground and trailhead parking area at the road's end.

Hiking directions: Cross Sespe Creek and the rocky creekbed, heading north to the posted trail junction. The left fork leads to the Piedra Blanca formations (Hike 4). Take the right fork and head downstream, parallel to the northern banks of Sespe Creek. In a half mile, the trail crosses Piedra Blanca Creek. After crossing, the trail narrows as it enters a canyon. Past the canyon, the trail widens out again and crosses Trout Creek. Along the way, side paths lead down to the creek. A short distance ahead, the trail enters the Sespe Wilderness. The trail gains elevation to a vista overlooking the canyon and passes through a gate. At the top of the ridge, the view opens up to the mountains in the north. The ridge is the turnaround spot.

To hike further, the trail follows Sespe Creek downstream for miles with numerous creek crossings. The first crossing is at Bear Canyon, 4.5 miles from the trailhead.

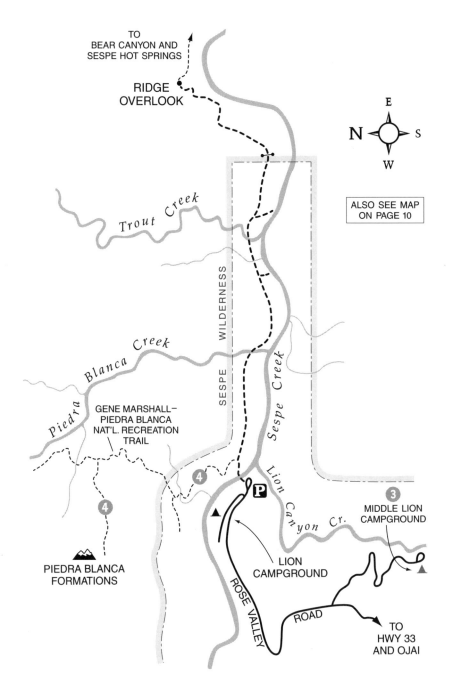

TO
BEAR CANYON AND
SESPE HOT SPRINGS

RIDGE
OVERLOOK

E
N ☼ S
W

ALSO SEE MAP
ON PAGE 10

Trout Creek

SESPE WILDERNESS

Piedra Blanca Creek

Sespe Creek

GENE MARSHALL–
PIEDRA BLANCA
NAT'L. RECREATION
TRAIL

4

4

Lion Canyon Cr.

P

3
MIDDLE LION
CAMPGROUND

PIEDRA BLANCA
FORMATIONS

LION
CAMPGROUND

ROSE VALLEY ROAD

TO
HWY 33
AND OJAI

SESPE RIVER TRAIL

Hike 6
Wheeler Gorge Nature Trail

Hiking distance: 1 mile loop
Hiking time: 30 minutes
Elevation gain: 200 feet
Maps: U.S.G.S. Wheeler Springs
Sespe Wilderness Trail Map

Summary of hike: Wheeler Gorge Nature Trail is an interpretive trail on the North Fork Matilija Creek near Wheeler Gorge Campground. The trail is an excellent introduction to the shaded creekside riparian habitats and arid chaparral plant communities that are so common throughout the area. The path winds through a small canyon gorge under sycamores, cottonwoods, willows and oaks, following the year-round creek past trickling waterfalls and bedrock pools. Free brochures from the Ojai Ranger Station correspond with numbered posts along the trail.

Driving directions: From Ojai, drive 8 miles north on Highway 33 (Maricopa Highway) to the Wheeler Gorge Campground on the left. Continue on the highway 0.5 miles to the posted nature trail on the left by a locked metal gate, just before crossing the bridge over the North Fork Matilija Creek.

Hiking directions: From the trailhead map panel, take the path to the right, following the North Fork Matilija Creek upstream. Cross under the Highway 33 bridge, passing cascades, small waterfalls and pools. Rock hop to the north side of the creek, and climb up through chaparral dotted with oaks. Follow the watercourse, passing a 12-foot waterfall between signposts 7 and 8. Cross over a rock formation, and wind through a shady tunnel of tall chaparral. Climb rock steps to a vista of Dry Lakes Ridge to the north. Curve away from the creekside vegetation, and descend on the northern slope of the arid hillside. Curve left and parallel Highway 33 from above. Drop back down to the creek, completing the loop. Recross the creek and return to the trailhead.

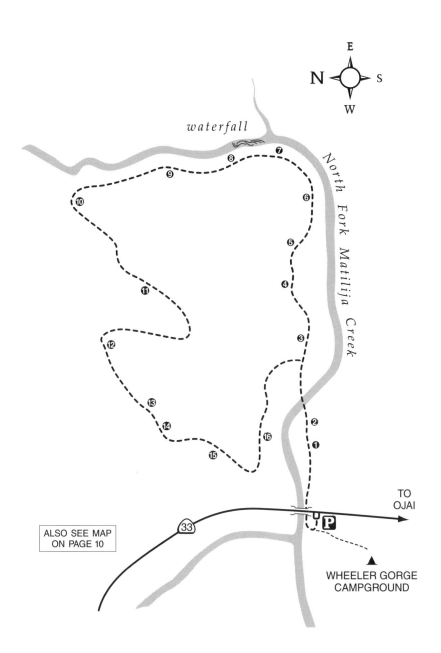

WHEELER GORGE
NATURE TRAIL

Hike 7
Murietta Canyon

Hiking distance: 3 miles round trip
Hiking time: 1.5 hours
Elevation gain: 200 feet
Maps: U.S.G.S. Old Man Mountain and White Ledge Peak

Summary of hike: The Murietta Trail begins in Matilija Canyon and enters Murietta Canyon en route. The trail follows Murietta Creek while heading to a campground on a beautiful, wooded flat. Murietta Camp sits at the edge of Murietta Creek under a forest canopy dominated by cedar and oak trees. There are cascades and pools at the creek.

Driving directions: From Ojai, drive 4.9 miles north on Highway 33 (Maricopa Highway) to Matilija Canyon Road and turn left. Continue 4.8 miles to the parking area on the left by the trailhead gate.

Hiking directions: From the parking area, follow the road past the gate and trailhead sign. Continue west along the unpaved road, crossing two streams. At 0.7 miles, a short distance past the second stream, is the signed Murietta Trail on the left. Leave the road and head south on the footpath towards the mouth of Murietta Canyon. Proceed to a stream crossing by pools and cascades. Rock hop across the stream channels and up a small hill, heading deeper into the canyon. Murietta Camp is at 1.7 miles. From the camp, several trails lead down to the stream. Return along the same path.

Up the canyon from the campground, the trail enters a dense forest with a tangle of vegetation and underbrush. This unmaintained trail becomes vague and hard to follow.

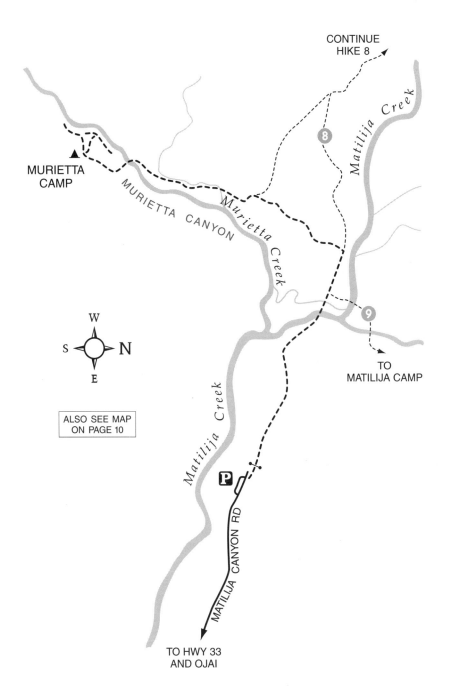

CONTINUE
HIKE 8

8

Matilija Creek

MURIETTA
CAMP

MURIETTA CANYON

Murietta Creek

9

TO
MATILIJA CAMP

W
S ✦ N
E

ALSO SEE MAP
ON PAGE 10

Matilija Creek

P

MATILIJA CANYON RD

TO HWY 33
AND OJAI

MURIETTA CANYON

Hike 8
Matilija Creek

Hiking distance: 7 miles round trip
Hiking time: 3 hours
Elevation gain: 600 feet
Maps: U.S.G.S. Old Man Mountain

Summary of hike: Matilija Creek leads up the main canyon to beautiful pools, cascades, and water slides. Large shale slabs border the creek for sunbathing beneath the steep canyon cliffs. Up canyon are several towering waterfalls.

Driving directions: From Ojai, drive 4.9 miles north on Highway 33 (Maricopa Highway) to Matilija Canyon Road and turn left. Continue 4.8 miles to the parking area on the left by the trailhead gate.

Hiking directions: Hike west up the road, past the gate and across two streams. Stay on the main road to an intersection with another trail at one mile. Take the right fork past a house on a Forest Service easement. For a short distance, the trail borders a beautiful rock wall. As you approach the mountain range, cross the stream and curve to the right. The trail follows the western edge of the deep, narrow canyon and crosses another stream. Climb up a short hill to a perch overlooking the canyon. Take the left fork that curves around the gully, and hike down the rocky drainage. Near the canyon floor, the trail picks up again to the left. Hike parallel to the creek along its endless cascades, pools, and rock slabs. This natural playground is the destination. Return along the same path.

To hike further, continue up canyon, creating your own path. There are several waterfalls ahead. Two are located another mile up the main canyon. Another falls is in the canyon to the northeast. This part of the hike is difficult due to slippery shale and an indistinct trail.

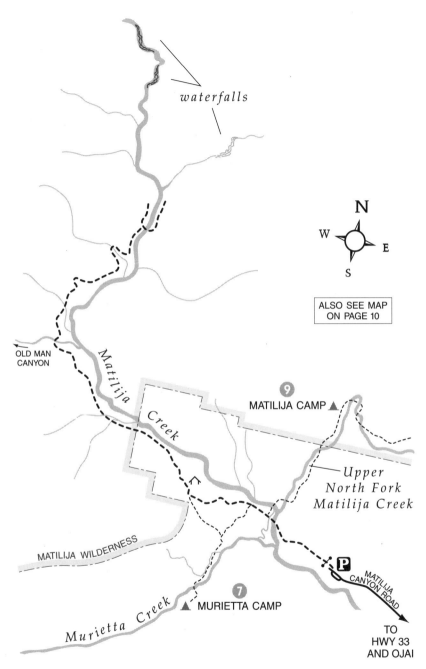

waterfalls

N
W E
S

ALSO SEE MAP
ON PAGE 10

OLD MAN
CANYON

Matilija

Creek

⑨ MATILIJA CAMP ▲

*Upper
North Fork
Matilija Creek*

MATILIJA WILDERNESS

P

MATILIJA
CANYON ROAD

▲ MURIETTA CAMP ⑦

Murietta Creek

TO
HWY 33
AND OJAI

MATILIJA CREEK

Hike 9
Matilija Camp Trail

Hiking distance: 2 miles round trip
Hiking time: 1 hour
Elevation gain: 200 feet
Maps: U.S.G.S. Old Man Mountain and Wheeler Springs

Summary of hike: The Matilija Camp Trail parallels the Upper North Fork of Matilija Creek in the Los Padres National Forest. The easy trail winds through the lush canyon in the shade of oaks and sycamores. There are three creek crossings en route to the Matilija Campsite, the destination for this hike. At the oak-shaded camp are large boulders, sandstone cliffs, swimming holes, pools and a picnic area.

Driving directions: From Ojai, drive 4.9 miles north on Highway 33 (Maricopa Highway) to Matilija Canyon Road and turn left. Continue 4.8 miles to the parking area on the left by the trailhead gate.

Hiking directions: From the parking area, walk up the unpaved road past the gate, a wildlife refuge and two creek crossings. At 0.5 miles, just past the second creek crossing, leave the road and take the signed Matilija Camp Trail to the right. The well-defined trail heads north, winding its way up the narrow canyon floor between steep, brown cliffs. Cross to the east side of the Upper North Fork Matilija Creek, entering the Matilija Wilderness. Matilija Camp and the pools are between the next two creek crossing. The camp is our turnaround spot.

To hike further, the trail leads to Middle Matilija Camp in another two miles. The trail to the middle camp has several more creek crossings and passes through a wide meadow.

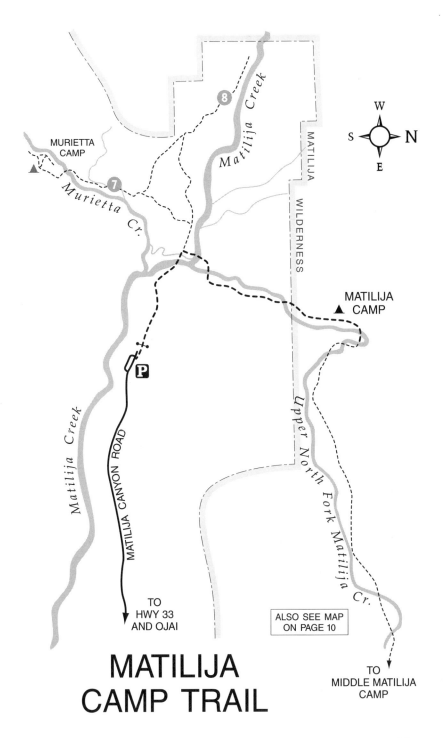

MURIETTA
CAMP

MATILIJA
WILDERNESS

MATILIJA
▲ CAMP

Matilija Creek

Murietta Cr.

Matilija Creek

P

MATILIJA CANYON ROAD

Upper North Fork Matilija Cr.

TO
HWY 33
AND OJAI

ALSO SEE MAP
ON PAGE 10

TO
MIDDLE MATILIJA
CAMP

MATILIJA
CAMP TRAIL

Hike 10
Cozy Dell Trail

Hiking distance: 4 miles round trip
Hiking time: 2 hours
Elevation gain: 700 feet
Maps: U.S.G.S. Matilija
Sespe Wilderness Trail Map

Summary of hike: The Cozy Dell Trail climbs up a small, shaded canyon to several vista points with panoramic views in every direction. There are great views into the Ojai Valley to the south and the surrounding peaks of the Santa Ynez and Topatopa Mountains. From the overlooks, the trail drops into the beautiful and forested Cozy Dell Canyon.

Driving directions: From Ojai, drive 3.4 miles north on Highway 33 (Maricopa Highway) to the Cozy Dell trailhead parking pullout on the left (west) side of the road. The pullout is located by a bridge, a packing house and a Forest Service trailhead sign.

Hiking directions: From the parking area, cross the highway to the trailhead, south of the packing house along the right side of the metal railing. Take the well-defined trail east, and head up the canyon. A short distance ahead is a series of 18 switchbacks, gaining 600 feet up the south edge of the canyon. At one mile, the trail reaches its peak at a saddle, giving way to an open area with breathtaking views. Proceed downhill towards Cozy Dell Canyon and back up to a second saddle with more outstanding views. The trail drops back into the trees, descending 200 feet into forested Cozy Dell Canyon, Cozy Dell Creek, and a T-junction with the Cozy Dell Road. One hundred yards to the left is a posted junction with the Foothill Trail (Hike 13). This is the turnaround spot. Return by retracing your steps.

To hike further, the fire road continues to the Pratt Trail and Foothill Fire Road at Stewart Canyon.

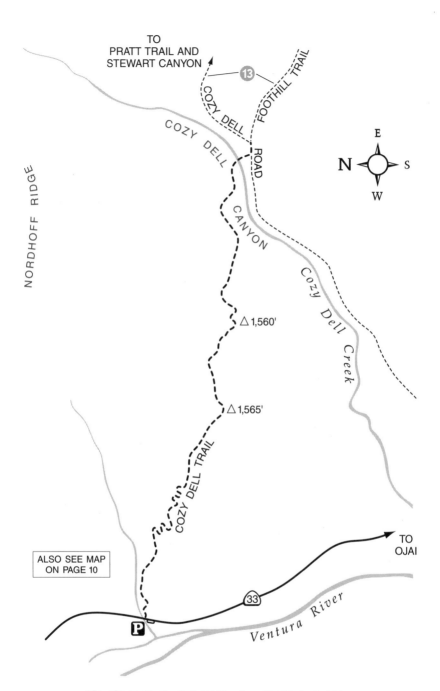

TO
PRATT TRAIL AND
STEWART CANYON

⑬

FOOTHILL TRAIL

COZY DELL

COZY DELL

ROAD

CANYON

Cozy Dell Creek

NORDHOFF RIDGE

E
N ☼ S
W

△1,560'

△1,565'

COZY DELL TRAIL

ALSO SEE MAP
ON PAGE 10

TO
OJAI

㉝

Ventura River

P

COZY DELL TRAIL

Hike 11
Shelf Road

Hiking distance: 3.5 miles round trip
Hiking time: 1.5 hours
Elevation gain: 200 feet
Maps: U.S.G.S. Ojai
       Sespe Wilderness Trail Map

Summary of hike: Shelf Road is an old, unpaved road that traverses the cliffs several hundred feet above the northern edge of Ojai. The road, connecting Signal Street with Gridley Road, is gated at both ends. It is a hiking, biking and jogging path that is popular with locals. The path has several scenic over-looks with views of the ten-mile long Ojai Valley, Sulphur Mountain across the valley, and the city of Ojai.

Driving directions: From downtown Ojai, drive one mile north up Signal Street (on the west side of the arcade) to the trailhead gate. Park along the side of the road.

Hiking directions: Hike north past the gate and up the abandoned road. The road curves east, passing orange trees and avocado groves. Shelf Road follows the contours of the cliffs, snaking its way to the east above the city. At 1.7 miles, the trail ends at another entrance gate by Gridley Road. Return to the trailhead along the same route.

For a longer hike, the Shelf Road hike may be combined with the Foothill–Gridley Loop (Hike 14). This loop hike is a back-country hike while Shelf Road is more of an easy social stroll.

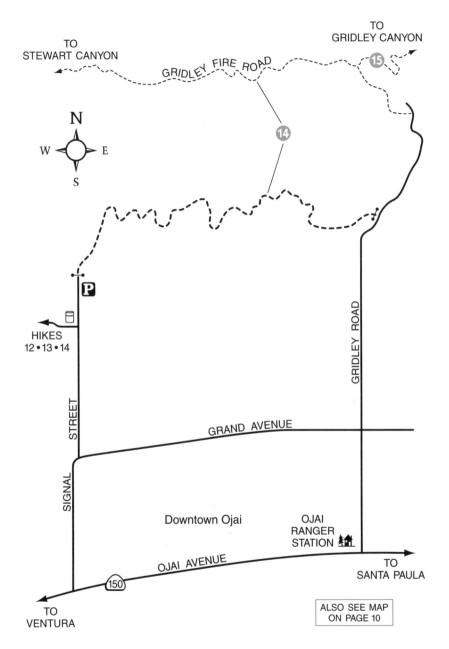

TO
STEWART CANYON

TO
GRIDLEY CANYON

GRIDLEY FIRE ROAD

N
W · E
S

14

15

P

HIKES
12 • 13 • 14

GRIDLEY ROAD

STREET

GRAND AVENUE

SIGNAL

Downtown Ojai

OJAI
RANGER
STATION

TO
SANTA PAULA

OJAI AVENUE

150

TO
VENTURA

ALSO SEE MAP
ON PAGE 10

SHELF ROAD

Hike 12
Stewart Canyon

Hiking distance: 2.6 miles round trip
Hiking time: 1.5 hours
Elevation gain: 600 feet
Maps: U.S.G.S. Ojai and Matilija
Sespe Wilderness Trail Map

Summary of hike: Stewart Canyon, at the north edge of Ojai, is the gateway to a network of magnificent hiking trails in the Los Padres National Forest. The canyon connects with the Foothill Trail to Cozy Dell Canyon (Hike 13), the Pratt Trail to Nordhoff Ridge, and the Gridley Fire Road to Gridley Canyon (Hike 14). This hike winds up the lower canyon, following Stewart Creek through a eucalyptus grove, meadows and landscaped rock gardens to a scenic vista across the Ojai Valley.

Driving directions: From downtown Ojai, drive 0.8 miles north up Signal Street (on the west side of the arcade) to the Pratt/Foothill Trailhead sign by the water tower. Turn left and drive 0.2 miles to the parking area on the left.

Hiking directions: Take the posted Pratt Trail, and curve north up Stewart Canyon. Parallel Stewart Creek to an unpaved road and junction. Continue straight ahead, following the trail sign. Weave through boulders on the distinct trail to a second junction. Take the left fork and walk through a eucalyptus grove, heading up the east wall of Stewart Canyon. At one mile, the trail reaches a plateau above the canyon with great views of the Ojai Valley. Descend into the canyon, staying on the trail past a few hillside homes, a creekside rock garden and a paved road crossing. Cross Stewart Creek and take the Foothill Fire Road to the right, following the "trail" signs. Continue along a beautiful rock wall. Pass a gate and water tank to the posted Pratt and Foothill Trail junction on the left (Hike 13). Stay on the main trail, and continue climbing a quarter mile to a Y-fork on a wide, rounded flat. This is our turnaround spot. The Gridley Fire

Road, also known as the Ojai Front Fuelbreak Road (Hike 14), bears right. The left fork continues to Nordhoff Peak and Cozy Dell Canyon.

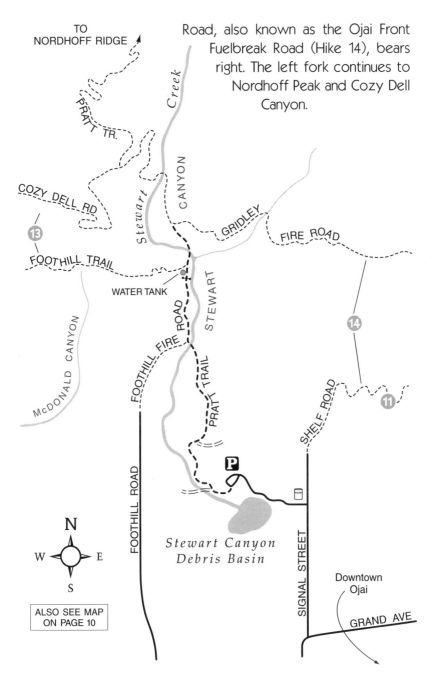

STEWART CANYON

Hike 13
Foothill Trail to Cozy Dell Canyon

Hiking distance: 5.8 mile loop
Hiking time: 3 hours
Elevation gain: 1,200 feet
Maps: U.S.G.S. Ojai and Matilija
      Sespe Wilderness Trail Map

Summary of hike: This loop hike follows Stewart Creek up the canyon, passing meadows and rock gardens to the Foothill Trail. The route heads west through McDonald Canyon and drops into pastoral Cozy Dell Canyon by the creek. Cozy Dell Road winds up the forested canyon, climbing to sweeping overlooks beneath Nordhoff Peak.

Driving directions: From downtown Ojai, drive 0.8 miles north up Signal Street (on the west side of the arcade) to the Pratt/Foothill Trailhead sign by the water tower. Turn left and drive 0.2 miles to the parking area on the left.

Hiking directions: Follow the hiking directions up Stewart Canyon—Hike 12—to the posted Pratt and Foothill Trail junction by the water tank. Begin the loop to the left and climb rock steps, ascending the east-facing hillside to a trail split. Curve left and continue uphill along short switchbacks with great views down Stewart Canyon and across Ojai Canyon to Sulphur Mountain. Cross a saddle to views of Lake Casitas and the Santa Ynez Mountains. Drop into McDonald Canyon and cross another saddle. Descend a sloping meadow bordered by oaks. Head into Cozy Dell Canyon to the Cozy Dell Road. (A hundred yards to the left is the Cozy Dell Trail—Hike 10.) Bear right on the fire road towards the posted Pratt Trail, meandering through the rolling forested glen. Steadily climb out of the canyon to a junction on a saddle. Bear left and continue uphill, curving right around the mountain to a posted junction with the Pratt Trail to Nordhoff Peak. Stay on the fire road to the right, and head downhill into Stewart Canyon to an open flat and road split. The left fork is the Gridley Fire Road (Hike 14). Descend to the right a quarter mile and complete the loop. Return down Stewart Canyon to the trailhead.

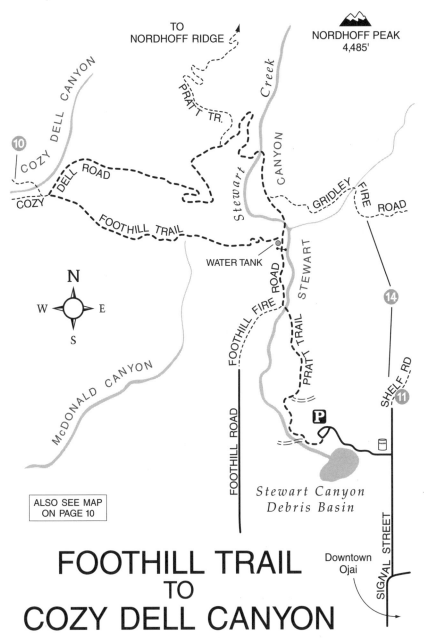

FOOTHILL TRAIL
TO
COZY DELL CANYON

Hike 14
Foothill Fire Road—Gridley Fire Road—
Shelf Road Loop

Hiking distance: 6.4 mile loop
Hiking time: 3.5 hours
Elevation gain: 900 feet
Maps: U.S.G.S. Ojai and Matilija
Sespe Wilderness Trail Map

Summary of hike: The Gridley Fire Road (Ojai Front Fuel-break Road) runs parallel to the Ojai Valley with stunning views a thousand feet above Ojai. The fire road connects Stewart Canyon on the west with Gridley Canyon on the east. This hike climbs up Stewart Canyon, traverses across the folded mountain layers to Gridley Road, and returns along Shelf Road. These fire roads are vehicle restricted.

Driving directions: From downtown Ojai, drive 0.8 miles north up Signal Street (on the west side of the arcade) to the Pratt/Foothill Trailhead sign by the water tower. Turn left and drive 0.2 miles to the parking area on the left.

Hiking directions: Follow the hiking directions for Hike 12 to the Gridley Fire Road junction—the turnaround point for Hike 12. At the junction, the left fork continues to Nordhoff Peak and Cozy Dell Canyon. Curve right on the Gridley Fire Road, and traverse the hillside on a winding course through the folded hills. Continue zigzagging eastward to a trail gate and posted junction on the right. The Gridley Trail (Hike 15) continues on the road to the left. Take the footpath to the right, and descend 0.4 miles to the top of Gridley Road. Follow Gridley Road downhill one-third mile to the Shelf Road trailhead on the right. Take Shelf Road and head west 1.7 miles to the Signal Street gate. The trailhead turnoff is 0.2 miles ahead by the water tower.

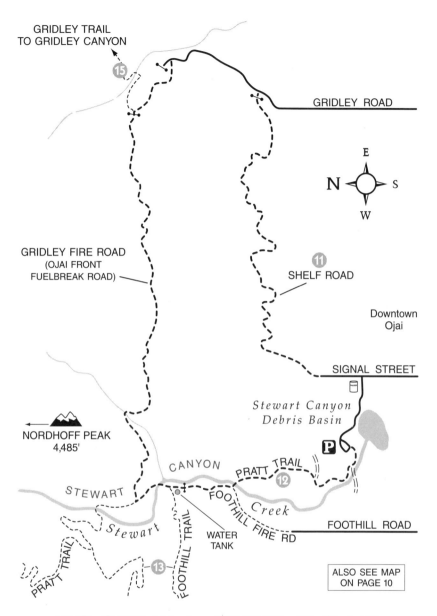

GRIDLEY TRAIL
TO GRIDLEY CANYON

⑮

GRIDLEY ROAD

N E S W

GRIDLEY FIRE ROAD
(OJAI FRONT
FUELBREAK ROAD)

⑪
SHELF ROAD

Downtown
Ojai

SIGNAL STREET

*Stewart Canyon
Debris Basin*

P

NORDHOFF PEAK
4,485'

CANYON

PRATT TRAIL

⑫

STEWART

FOOTHILL TRAIL

Creek

Stewart

FOOTHILL FIRE RD

FOOTHILL ROAD

WATER
TANK

PRATT TRAIL

⑬

FOOTHILL TRAIL

ALSO SEE MAP
ON PAGE 10

FOOTHILL FIRE ROAD
GRIDLEY FIRE ROAD
SHELF ROAD

Hike 15
Gridley Trail
to Gridley Springs Camp

Hiking distance: 6 miles round trip
Hiking time: 3 hours
Elevation gain: 1,200 feet
Maps: U.S.G.S. Ojai
　　　　Sespe Wilderness Trail Map

Summary of hike: The Gridley Trail begins at the edge of Ojai in the foothills of the Topatopa Mountains. The trail follows a fire road into Gridley Canyon along the shady northwest side. Gridley Trail eventually leads six miles up to Nordhoff Peak. This hike goes to Gridley Springs Camp, a primitive campsite by a stream that is halfway to the peak.

Driving directions: From downtown Ojai, drive one mile east on Highway 150 (Ojai Avenue) to Gridley Road and turn left. Continue 1.5 miles to the end of Gridley Road, and park by the signed trailhead on the left.

Hiking directions: Take the signed trail on the west up a draw through the tall, native brush. Continue 0.4 miles to the Gridley Fire Road (Hike 14). There is a beautiful overlook of the Ojai Valley and Sulphur Mountain on the right. Head to the right up the unpaved, vehicle-restricted fire road past avocado orchards on the steep slopes. The road curves around the contours of the mountain to a signed five-way junction in Gridley Canyon. Take the center left fork, following the trail sign. At two miles, the trail is perched high above the deep canyon and enters a small side canyon at the confluence of two streams. Gridley Springs Camp is at the first sharp switchback by a horse watering trough. This is the turnaround spot.

To hike further, the trail continues up switchbacks for three steep miles, gaining over 2,000 feet to Nordhoff Peak.

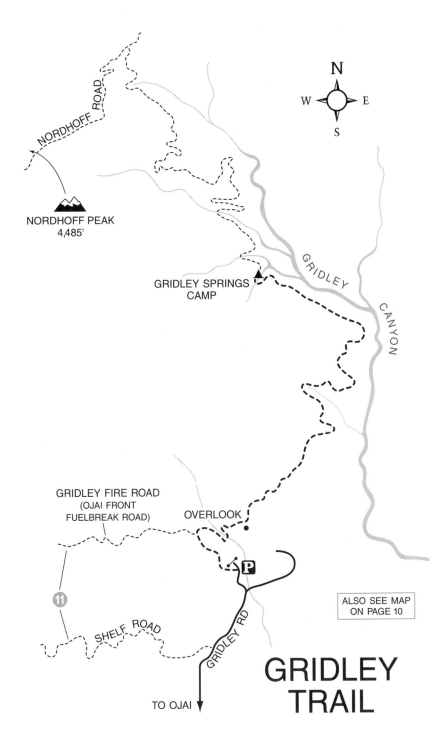

NORDHOFF ROAD

N
W E
S

NORDHOFF PEAK
4,485'

GRIDLEY SPRINGS
CAMP

GRIDLEY

CANYON

GRIDLEY FIRE ROAD
(OJAI FRONT
FUELBREAK ROAD)

OVERLOOK

11

SHELF ROAD

GRIDLEY RD

P

ALSO SEE MAP
ON PAGE 10

GRIDLEY
TRAIL

TO OJAI

Hike 16
Horn Canyon Trail

Hiking distance: 3 miles round trip
Hiking time: 1.5 hours
Elevation gain: 600 feet
Maps: U.S.G.S. Ojai
        Sespe Wilderness Trail Map

Summary of hike: The Horn Canyon Trail parallels Thacher Creek through a forested canyon that is lush with sycamores, alders and oaks. The trail, which is partially a service road, crosses the creek four times to a rocky gorge. At the gorge, the trail is rugged and far less used, leading past a continuous series of cascades, pools and small waterfalls.

Driving directions: From downtown Ojai, drive 2.3 miles east on Highway 150 (Ojai Avenue) to Reeves Road and turn left. Continue 1.1 mile to McAndrew Road and turn left again. Drive one mile and enter the Thacher School grounds. The trailhead parking area is 0.4 miles ahead, bearing right at all three road splits.

Hiking directions: From the parking area, take the unpaved service road northeast past the gate and kiosk into Horn Canyon. There are two creek crossings in the first half mile. After the second crossing, the service road enters the forest and the trail narrows. At one mile, the trail crosses the creek again and climbs up the west wall of the canyon. There are great views of Horn Canyon and the creek below. Just before the fourth creek crossing, leave the main trail and take the left path, heading up Horn Canyon along the west side of the creek. The trail is replaced by faint paths that crisscross the creek in a scramble past pools, cascades and small waterfalls. Choose your own turnaround spot, and return along the same path.

To hike further, at the fourth creek crossing, continue on the Horn Canyon Trail across the creek. The trail steeply climbs out of the canyon to the Pines Campsite one mile ahead.

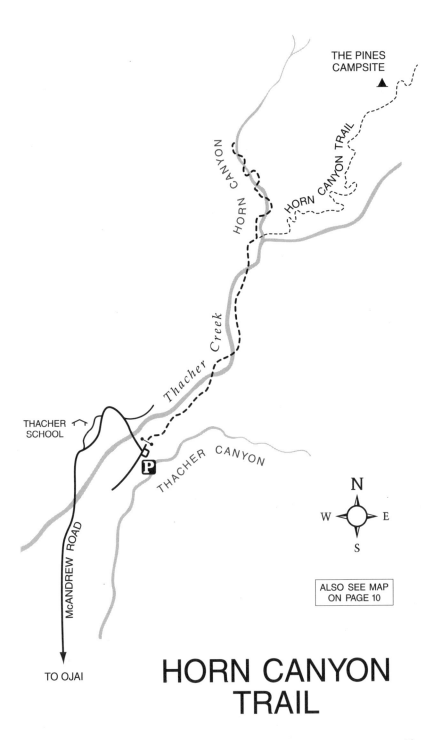

THE PINES
CAMPSITE

HORN CANYON

HORN CANYON TRAIL

Thacher Creek

THACHER
SCHOOL

THACHER CANYON

P

N

W · E

S

ALSO SEE MAP
ON PAGE 10

McANDREW ROAD

TO OJAI

HORN CANYON
TRAIL

Hike 17
Sulphur Mountain Road Recreation Trail

Hiking distance: 10 miles one way (shuttle)
Hiking time: 4 hours
Elevation loss: 2,200 feet
Maps: U.S.G.S. Ojai and Matilija
   Sespe Wilderness Trail Map

Summary of hike: Sulphur Mountain Road, a gated hiking, biking and equestrian road, follows a 2,600-foot ridge along Sulphur Mountain. This hike is a downhill walk from the trailhead to the shuttle car. The journey across the ridgeline has gorgeous alternating views. There are views to the south and west of the Conejo Valley, the Pacific Ocean and the Channel Islands. At other times there are views to the north of the Ojai Valley, the Topatopa Mountains and the Los Padres National Forest.

Driving directions: Leave a shuttle car at the end of the hike: From Highway 101/Ventura Freeway in Ventura, drive 7.5 miles north on Highway 33 towards Ojai to Sulphur Mountain Road and turn right. Continue 0.4 miles to the locked gate. Park the shuttle car alongside the road.

   To the trailhead: Return to Highway 33 and continue north to Ojai. From downtown Ojai, drive 6.4 miles east on Highway 150 towards Santa Paula. Turn right on Sulphur Mountain Road, and continue 4.6 miles up the winding road to a locked gate at the trailhead.

Hiking directions: From the locked gate, hike west along the paved road. At about 1.5 miles, the pavement ends. Continue west along the gradual but steady downhill trail along the mountain ridge. The last two miles are steeper, dropping 1,500 feet. As you near the trail's end, the winding road descends past a cattle guard and gate to the shuttle car parking area at Casitas Springs.

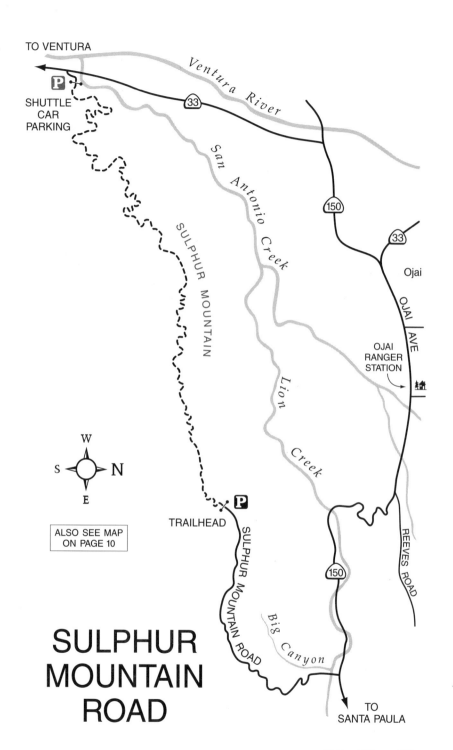

TO VENTURA

P

SHUTTLE
CAR
PARKING

Ventura River

33

San Antonio Creek

SULPHUR MOUNTAIN

150

33

Ojai

OJAI AVE

OJAI
RANGER
STATION

Lion

Creek

W

S ⊕ N

E

ALSO SEE MAP
ON PAGE 10

TRAILHEAD

P

SULPHUR MOUNTAIN ROAD

REEVES ROAD

150

Big Canyon

SULPHUR
MOUNTAIN
ROAD

TO
SANTA PAULA

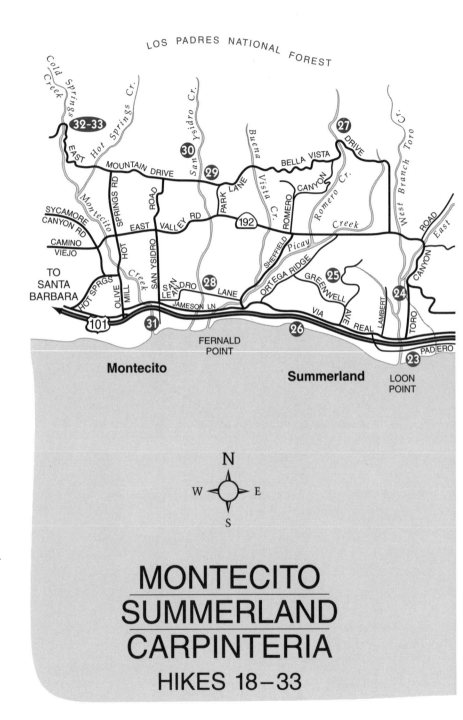

MONTECITO
SUMMERLAND
CARPINTERIA
HIKES 18–33

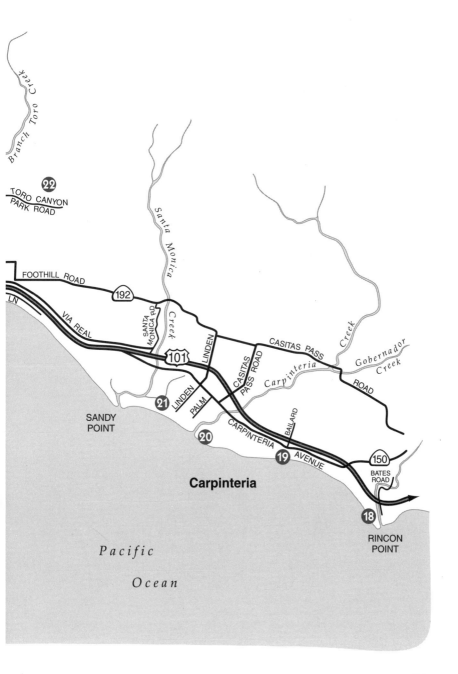

22 TORO CANYON PARK ROAD

Branch Toro Creek

Santa Monica Creek

FOOTHILL ROAD

192

VIA REAL

LN

SANTA MONICA RD

LINDEN

101

CASITAS PASS

Carpinteria Creek

Gobernador Creek

ROAD

21 LINDEN

PALM

CASITAS PASS ROAD

SANDY POINT

20

CARPINTERIA

BALLARD

19 AVENUE

150

Carpinteria

BATES ROAD

18

RINCON POINT

Pacific

Ocean

Hike 18
Rincon Point and Rincon Beach Park

Hiking distance: 2 miles round trip
Hiking time: 1 hour
Elevation gain: 100 feet
Maps: U.S.G.S. White Ledge Peak
       The Thomas Guide—Santa Barbara and Vicinity

Summary of hike: Rincon Point is a popular surfing spot with tidepools and a small bay. The point straddles the Santa Barbara/Ventura County line. Rincon Beach Park is on the west side of the point. The park sits on the steep, forested bluff with eucalyptus trees and Monterey pines. There is a large picnic area, great views of the coastline and a stairway to the 1,200 feet of beach frontage.

Driving directions: From Santa Barbara, drive southbound on Highway 101 for 3 miles past Carpinteria, and take the Bates Road exit to the stop sign. Park in either of the lots for Rincon Point or Rincon Park.

Hiking directions: Begin from the Rincon Park parking lot on the right (west). From the edge of the cliffs, a long staircase and a paved service road both lead down the cliff face, providing access to the sandy shoreline and tidepools. Walk north along the beach, strolling past a series of tidepools along the base of the sandstone cliffs. After beachcombing, return to the parking lot. From the west end of the parking lot, a well-defined trail heads west past the metal gate. The path is a wide shelf cut on the steep cliffs high above the ocean. At 0.3 miles, the trail reaches the railroad tracks. The path parallels the railroad right-of-way west to Carpinteria. Choose your own turnaround spot.

From the Rincon Point parking lot on the east, take the wide beach access path. Descend through a shady, forested grove to the beach. Bear right on the rocky path to a small bay near the tree-lined point. This is an excellent area to explore the tidepools and watch the surfers. Return the way you came.

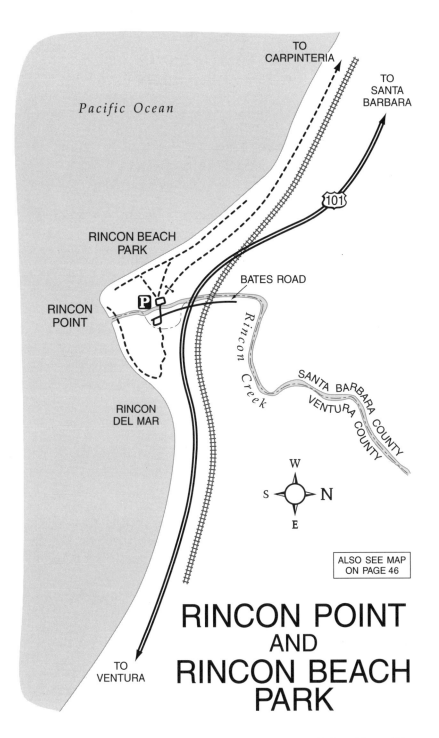

TO
CARPINTERIA

TO
SANTA
BARBARA

Pacific Ocean

101

RINCON BEACH
PARK

BATES ROAD

P

RINCON
POINT

Rincon Creek

RINCON
DEL MAR

SANTA BARBARA COUNTY
VENTURA COUNTY

W

S ✦ N

E

ALSO SEE MAP
ON PAGE 46

TO
VENTURA

RINCON POINT
AND
RINCON BEACH
PARK

Hike 19
Carpinteria Bluffs
and Seal Sanctuary

Hiking distance: 2 miles round trip
Hiking time: 1 hour
Elevation gain: Level
Maps: U.S.G.S. White Ledge Peak and Carpinteria
       The Thomas Guide—Santa Barbara & Vicinity

Summary of hike: The Carpinteria Bluffs and Seal Sanctuary are located in an incredible area along the Pacific. The bluffs encompass 52 oceanside acres with grasslands and eucalyptus groves. The area has panoramic views from the Santa Ynez Mountains to the islands of Anacapa, Santa Cruz and Santa Rosa. At the cliff's edge, 100 feet above the ocean, is an overlook of the seal sanctuary. Below, a community of harbor seals plays in the water, lounging and sunbathing on the rocks and shoreline. The sanctuary is a protected birthing habitat for harbor seals during the winter and spring from December 1 through May 31. Beach access is prohibited during these months, but the seals may be watched from the blufftop.

Driving directions: From Highway 101 in Carpinteria, exit on Bailard Avenue. Drive one block south towards the ocean, and park at the road's end.

Hiking directions: From the end of the road, hike south on the well-worn path across the open meadow towards the ocean. As you near the ocean cliffs, take the pathway to the right, parallel to a row of stately eucalyptus trees. At the west end of the eucalyptus grove, bear left and cross the railroad tracks. The trail resumes across the tracks, heading to the right. (For an optional side trip, take the beach access trail on the left down to the base of the cliffs.) Continue west along the edge of the ocean bluffs to a bamboo fence—the seal sanctuary overlook. After enjoying the seals and views, return along the same path.

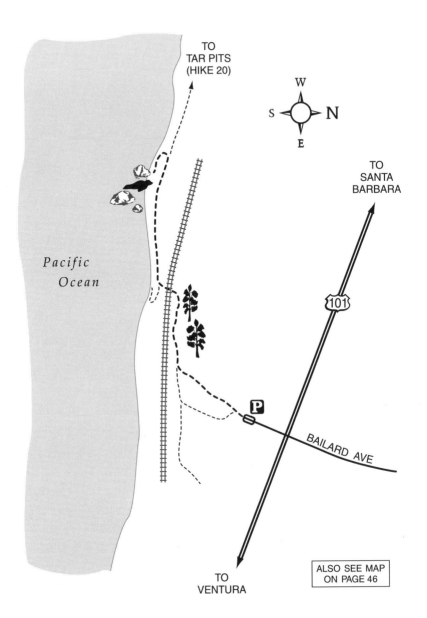

TO
TAR PITS
(HIKE 20)

W
S ◇ N
E

TO
SANTA
BARBARA

*Pacific
Ocean*

101

P

BAILARD AVE

ALSO SEE MAP
ON PAGE 46

TO
VENTURA

CARPINTERIA BLUFFS
AND
SEAL SANCTUARY

Hike 20
Tarpits Park

Hiking distance: 1.5 miles round trip
Hiking time: 1 hour
Elevation gain: 50 feet
Maps: U.S.G.S. Carpinteria

Summary of hike: Tarpits Park is an 8-acre blufftop park at the east end of Carpinteria State Beach. The park was once the site of a Chumash Indian village. It is named for the natural tar that seeps up from beneath the soil. The Indians used the tar for caulking canoes and sealing cooking vessels. Interconnecting trails cross the bluffs overlooking the steep, jagged coastline. Benches are placed along the edge of the bluffs.

Driving directions: From Highway 101 in Carpinteria, exit on Linden Avenue. Turn right and drive 0.5 miles south to Sixth Street. Turn left and go 0.2 miles to Palm Avenue. Turn right and drive one block to the Carpinteria State Beach parking lot on the right. A parking fee is required.

Hiking directions: Two routes lead to Tarpits Park. Either follow the sandy beach east, or walk along the campground road east, crossing over Carpinteria Creek. At a half mile, the campground road ends on the grassy bluffs. From the beach, a footpath ascends the bluffs to the campground road. Several interconnecting paths cross the clifftop terrace. The meandering trails pass groves of eucalyptus trees and Monterey pines. A stairway leads down to the shoreline. As you near the Chevron Oil Pier, the bluffs narrow. This is a good turnaround spot.

To hike further, cross the ravine and continue past the pier along the edge of the cliffs. You will reach the Carpinteria Bluffs and Seal Sanctuary (Hike 19) in a half mile.

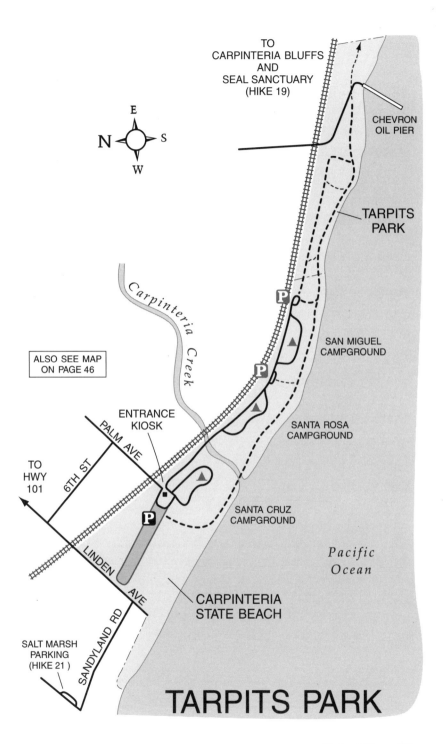

TO
CARPINTERIA BLUFFS
AND
SEAL SANCTUARY
(HIKE 19)

E
N S
W

CHEVRON
OIL PIER

TARPITS
PARK

Carpinteria Creek

ALSO SEE MAP
ON PAGE 46

P

SAN MIGUEL
CAMPGROUND

P

SANTA ROSA
CAMPGROUND

ENTRANCE
KIOSK

PALM AVE

TO
HWY
101

6TH ST

P

SANTA CRUZ
CAMPGROUND

Pacific
Ocean

LINDEN AVE

CARPINTERIA
STATE BEACH

SANDYLAND RD

SALT MARSH
PARKING
(HIKE 21)

TARPITS PARK

Hike 21
Salt Marsh Nature Park

Hiking distance: 1 mile round trip
Hiking time: 30 minutes
Elevation gain: Level
Maps: U.S.G.S. Carpinteria
       The Thomas Guide—Santa Barbara and Vicinity

Summary of hike: The Carpinteria Salt Marsh, historically known as El Estero (the estuary), is one of California's last remaining wetlands. The area was once inhabited by Chumash Indians. The 230-acre marsh is fed by Franklin Creek and Santa Monica Creek. The marsh has an abundance of sea and plant life and is a nesting ground for thousands of migratory waterfowl and shorebirds. The Salt Marsh Nature Park sits along the east end of the salt marsh with a trail system and several observation decks.

Driving directions: From Highway 101 in Carpinteria, exit on Linden Avenue. Turn right and drive 0.6 miles south to Sandyland Road, the last corner before reaching the ocean. Turn right and continue 0.2 miles to Ash Avenue. Park alongside the road by the signed park.

Hiking directions: From the nature trail sign, walk 20 yards to the west, reaching an observation deck. A boardwalk to the left leads to the ocean. Take the wide, meandering path to the right, parallel to Ash Avenue and the salt marsh. At the north end of the park, curve left to another overlook of the wetland. At the T-junction, the left fork leads a short distance to another observation deck. The right fork follows a pole fence along Franklin Creek to the trail's end. Return along the same path.

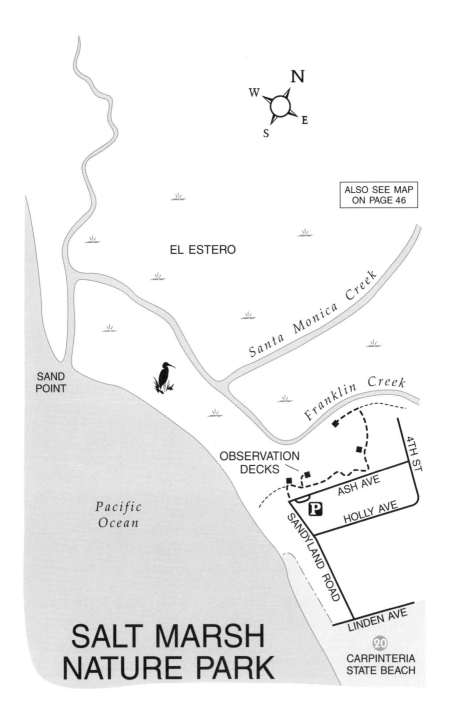

N
W   E
S

ALSO SEE MAP
ON PAGE 46

EL ESTERO

Santa Monica Creek

Franklin Creek

SAND
POINT

4TH ST

OBSERVATION
DECKS

ASH AVE

HOLLY AVE

P

SANDYLAND ROAD

Pacific
Ocean

LINDEN AVE

20
CARPINTERIA
STATE BEACH

SALT MARSH
NATURE PARK

Hike 22
Toro Canyon Park

Hiking distance: 1 mile round trip
Hiking time: 30 minutes
Elevation gain: 300 feet
Maps: U.S.G.S. Carpinteria
The Thomas Guide—Santa Barbara & Vicinity

Summary of hike: Toro Canyon Park, located in the foothills between Carpinteria and Summerland, takes in 74 acres of oak woodland, native chaparral and sandstone outcroppings. There are shady picnic spots under the trees and along the stream. The hike circles a knoll and heads up to a gazebo with panoramic 360-degree views of the coastline, mountains and orchards.

Driving directions: From Santa Barbara, drive southbound on Highway 101 to Summerland, and exit on North Padaro Lane. Drive north one block to Via Real and turn right. Continue 0.4 miles to Toro Canyon Road and turn left. Drive 1.3 miles to the signed Toro Canyon Park turnoff and turn right. Proceed one mile to Toro Canyon Park on the left. Turn left and drive 0.2 miles to the trail sign at the upper end of the park. Park by the sandstone outcropping on the right.

Hiking directions: From the parking area, hike north past the trail sign and across the stream towards the prominent sandstone formation. From the outcropping, take the wide, uphill path to the right. At 0.3 miles is a trail split, which is the beginning of the loop. Hiking clockwise, take the left fork around the small knoll and up to a gazebo at the hilltop. The vistas extend across the Montecito foothills to the Carpinteria plain and Ventura. After enjoying the beautiful views, continue to the west, completing the loop around the hill. Return to the left, back to the trailhead.

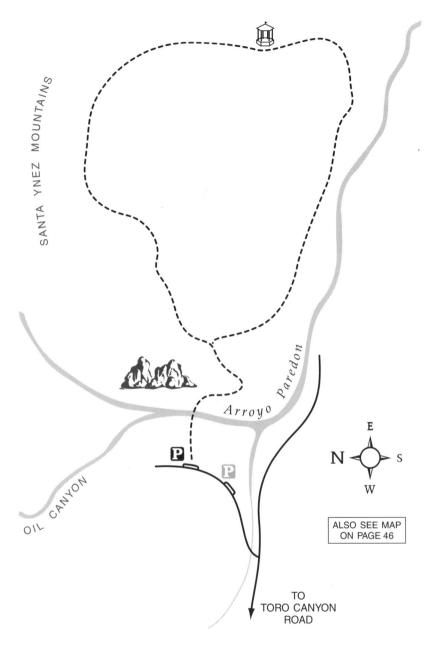

SANTA YNEZ MOUNTAINS

Arroyo Paredon

OIL CANYON

P

P

E
N ✧ S
W

ALSO SEE MAP
ON PAGE 46

TO
TORO CANYON
ROAD

TORO CANYON PARK

Hike 23
Loon Point

Hiking distance: 3 miles round trip
Hiking time: 1.5 hours
Elevation gain: Near level
Maps: U.S.G.S. Carpinteria
　　　　The Thomas Guide—Santa Barbara and Vicinity

Summary of hike: Loon Point sits between Summerland and Carpinteria at the mouth of Toro Canyon Creek. Dense stands of sycamores, coastal oaks, Monterey cypress and eucalypti line the creek. The path to Loon Point follows an isolated stretch of coastline along the base of steep 40-foot sandstone cliffs.

Driving directions: From Santa Barbara, drive southbound on Highway 101 to Summerland, and exit on Padero Lane south. Turn right and drive 0.2 miles to the signed Loon Point Beach parking lot on the left.

Hiking directions: Take the signed Loon Beach access trail parallel to the railroad tracks. Curve to the left, under the Padero Lane bridge, past a grove of eucalyptus trees. The path descends through a narrow drainage between the jagged, weathered cliffs to the shoreline. Bear to the right on the sandy beach along the base of the sandstone cliffs. Loon Point can be seen jutting out to sea. Follow the shoreline, reaching large boulders at Loon Point in 1.5 miles. At high tide, the water level may be too high to reach the point. At a lower tide, the beach walk can be extended from Loon Point to Lookout Park, 1.5 miles west (Hike 26).

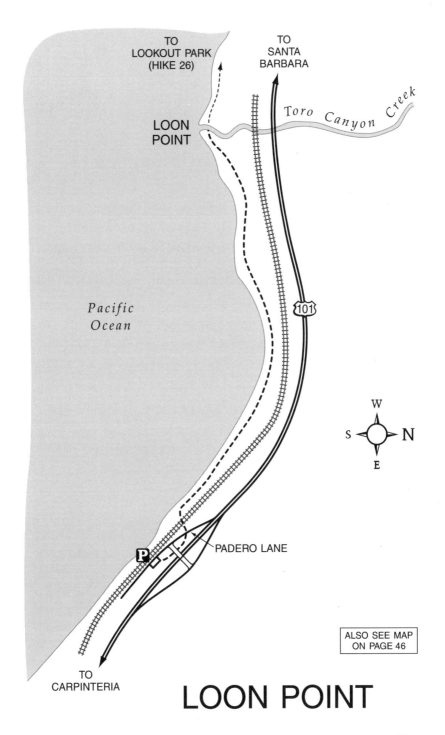

TO
LOOKOUT PARK
(HIKE 26)

TO
SANTA
BARBARA

Toro Canyon Creek

LOON
POINT

Pacific Ocean

101

W
S — N
E

PADERO LANE

P

ALSO SEE MAP
ON PAGE 46

TO
CARPINTERIA

LOON POINT

Hike 24
Polo Club—Toro Canyon Creek Trails

Hiking distance: 3.2 miles round trip
Hiking time: 1.5 hours
Elevation gain: 200 feet
Maps: U.S.G.S. Carpinteria
Montecito Trails Foundation Trails Map

map next page

Summary of hike: The Montecito Trail Foundation preserves and maintains a vast network of trails throughout Montecito, Summerland and Carpinteria. Polo Club Trail and Toro Canyon Creek Trail are two of these scenic routes that meander through the forested foothills of Summerland. The Toro Canyon Creek Trail follows the creek through an enchanting forest of oaks and sycamores. The Polo Club Trail connects Toro Canyon with Greenwell Road, climbing to a large lemon orchard with an overlook of Summerland, Carpenteria and the Pacific Ocean.

Driving directions: From Highway 101 in Summerland, exit on North Padero Lane. Cross over the freeway a half block, and turn right on Via Real. Drive 0.5 miles to Toro Canyon Road and turn left. Continue 0.5 miles north to the posted trailhead on the left next to a private road and a utility pole. Park in the small pullouts on the side of the road.

Hiking directions: Head west on the signed trail along the left side of the gravel driveway. Follow the forested Polo Club Trail under the shade of oak trees, crossing Garrapato Creek. Merge with the gravel road for 40 yards, and return to the footpath on the left, crossing a rocky streambed to a trail split. Take Toro Canyon Creek Trail to the left, and curve around the Spanish style stucco home. Head south through a large grove of sycamores and twisted oaks draped in vinca vines. The meandering path crosses Toro Canyon Creek twice and emerges from the forest to the polo field. Follow the east edge of the expansive grassy lawn, parallel to Toro Canyon Creek. The trail ends by a bamboo grove at Via Real, just west of the Toro

Canyon Creek bridge. Return to the junction with the Polo Club Trail. Bear left on the Polo Club Trail, and skirt the north boundary of the horse ranch through a forest of oak and eucalyptus trees to Lambert Road. Bear left and follow the tree-lined road 200 yards to the posted trail on the right, just after crossing the stone bridge. Follow the fenced trail corridor through a horse ranch, and ascend the hillside into a lemon orchard. Follow the trail signs to the upper level of the orchard, weaving clockwise through the orchard to an unpaved road. Drop down to the Greenwell Preserve on Asegra Road by Greenwell Avenue and the Reservoir Trail (Hike 25). Return by retracing your steps.

Hike 25
Reservoir—Edison Loop

Hiking distance: 1.7 mile loop
Hiking time: 1 hour
Elevation gain: 300 feet
Maps: U.S.G.S. Carpinteria
       Montecito Trails Foundation Trails Map

map
next page

Summary of hike: The Reservoir and Edison Trails, located in the Summerland Greenwell Preserve, climb a small stream-fed canyon to an overlook at the Ortega Reservoir. These two trails are part of a network of interwoven trails connecting Montecito, Summerland and Carpinteria. The trail system is preserved and maintained by the Montecito Trail Foundation, supported entirely by membership dues and donations: (805) 969-3514.

Driving directions: From Highway 101 in Summerland, exit on North Padero Lane. Cross over the freeway a half block, and turn left on Via Real. Drive 0.5 miles to Greenwell Avenue and turn right. Continue 0.3 miles north to the Greenwell Preserve parking lot on the left by the railroad tie fence.

Hiking directions: Walk up the road past the block buildings to the large "Private Road" sign. Bear left on the gravel road to the posted footpath and trailhead gate. Head west up the draw on the tree-lined path to a trail split at 200 yards. Begin the loop on the Reservoir Trail to the right. Cross a seasonal stream through a willow thicket, and ascend the hillside on the north canyon wall. Climb to an overlook of the Pacific Ocean and Channel Islands on Ortega Ridge. Drop down from the ridge at the south edge of the Ortega Reservoir, and climb two switchbacks to Hunt Drive. Bear left, follow the paved road around the reservoir, and descend to Ortega Ridge Road. (Across the road is the posted Valley Club Trail which drops down the hillside to Sheffield Drive.) Bear left 30 yards on Ortega Ridge Road to the posted Edison Trail on the left. Descend on the wide gravel path, dropping into the canyon and completing the loop.

Picay

SHEFFIELD DRIVE

VALLEY CLUB TRAIL

ORTEGA RIDGE ROAD

ORTEGA HILL ROAD

TO SANTA BARBARA

JAMESON LANE

EVANS AVE

101

26 LOOKOUT PARK

HIKE 24
POLO CLUB TRAIL
TORO CANYON CREEK TRAIL

HIKE 25
RESERVOIR TRAIL
EDISON TRAIL

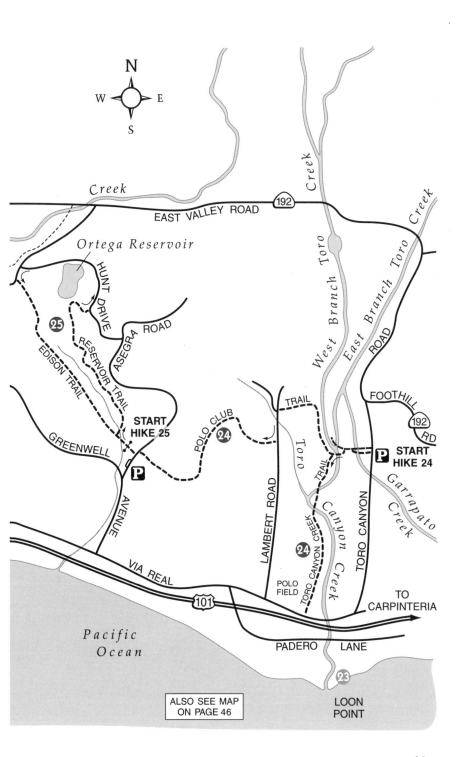

N
W E
S

Creek

Creek

192

EAST VALLEY ROAD

Ortega Reservoir

HUNT DRIVE

ASEGRA ROAD

RESERVOIR TRAIL

EDISON TRAIL

25

GREENWELL

AVENUE

START HIKE 25

POLO CLUB

24

TRAIL

West Branch Toro

East Branch Toro Creek

ROAD

FOOTHILL

192

RD

P START HIKE 24

Garrapato Creek

Toro Canyon Creek

Canyon Creek

TRAIL

TORO CANYON

P

LAMBERT ROAD

VIA REAL

101

POLO FIELD

24

TORO CANYON CREEK

TO CARPINTERIA

PADERO LANE

Pacific Ocean

23

LOON POINT

ALSO SEE MAP ON PAGE 46

Hike 26
Summerland Beach
from Lookout Park

Hiking distance: 1 mile loop
Hiking time: 30 minutes
Elevation gain: 50 feet
Maps: U.S.G.S. Carpinteria
       The Thomas Guide—Santa Barbara & Vicinity

Summary of hike: Lookout Park is a beautiful grassy flat along the oceanfront cliffs in Summerland. From the 4-acre park perched above the sea, paved walkways and natural forested trails lead down to a sandy beach, creating a one-mile loop. There are tidepools and coves a short distance up the coast from the beach.

Driving directions: From Santa Barbara, drive southbound on Highway 101 and take the Summerland exit. Turn right (south), crossing the railroad tracks in one block, and park in the Lookout Park parking lot.

From the south, heading northbound on Highway 101, take the Evans Avenue exit and turn left. Cross Highway 101 and the railroad tracks to Lookout Park.

Hiking directions: From the parking lot, head left (east) through the grassy flat along the cliff's edge to an open gate. A path leads through a shady eucalyptus tree forest. Cross a wooden bridge, and head to the sandy shoreline. At the shore, bear to the right, leading to the paved walkways that return up to Lookout Park. To extend the hike, continue along the coastline to the west. At low tide, the long stretch of beach leads to coves, rocky points and tidepools.

The beach continues west past charming beachfront homes, reaching Eucalyptus Lane and the Hammonds Meadow Trailhead (Hike 31) at 2 miles. From Lookout Park, the beach heads 1.5 miles east to Loon Point (Hike 23).

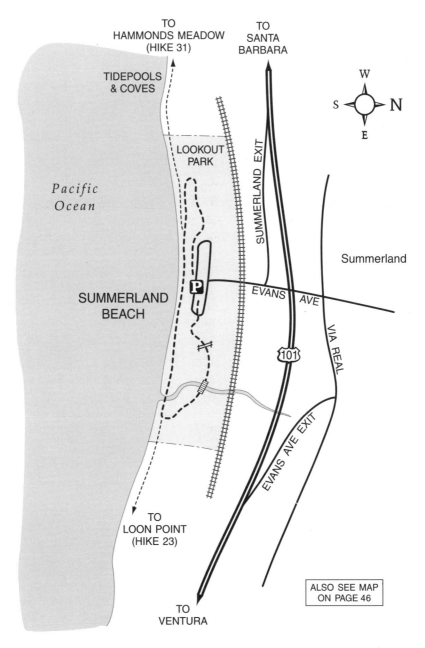

TO
HAMMONDS MEADOW
(HIKE 31)

TO
SANTA
BARBARA

TIDEPOOLS
& COVES

W

S — N

E

LOOKOUT
PARK

*Pacific
Ocean*

SUMMERLAND EXIT

Summerland

P

EVANS   AVE

SUMMERLAND
BEACH

VIA REAL

101

TO
LOON POINT
(HIKE 23)

EVANS AVE EXIT

ALSO SEE MAP
ON PAGE 46

TO
VENTURA

SUMMERLAND BEACH
FROM LOOKOUT PARK

Hike 27
Romero Canyon Loop

Hiking distance: 6 mile loop
Hiking time: 3 hours
Elevation gain: 1,400 feet
Maps: U.S.G.S. Carpinteria
          Santa Barbara Front Country Recreational Map

Summary of hike: The Romero Canyon Trail follows Romero Creek up a narrow, shady, secluded canyon past pools and a waterfall. The hike returns on scenic Romero Canyon Road, an abandoned road with dramatic vistas that overlook the canyon and the coastline.

Driving directions: From Santa Barbara, drive southbound on Highway 101, and exit on Sheffield Drive in Montecito. Turn right and drive 1.3 miles to East Valley Road. Turn left and quickly turn right on Romero Canyon Road. Continue 1.5 miles (bearing right at 0.4 miles) to Bella Vista Drive and turn right. Drive a quarter mile to a horseshoe bend in the road. The trailhead is at this bend on the left by a steel gate.

Hiking directions: Hike past the gate on old Romero Road along the east side of Romero Creek. After a quarter mile, cross the wide concrete bridge over the creek. At 0.4 miles is a second creek crossing and a junction. The left fork leads west to San Ysidro Canyon. Head right on the main trail to another creek crossing a hundred yards ahead. After crossing, begin the loop. Leave the main trail and take the left fork, following the trail sign up the secluded Romero Canyon. The trail runs parallel to the creek, crossing boulders by pools and a waterfall at 1.3 miles. A short distance ahead, two streams converge and the trail crosses the stream. At 1.7 miles, switchbacks lead up to Romero Canyon Road. Take the road to the right, beginning a four-mile descent with dramatic views overlooking the canyon and coast. Complete the loop at the canyon junction and creek crossing. Retrace your steps back to the trailhead.

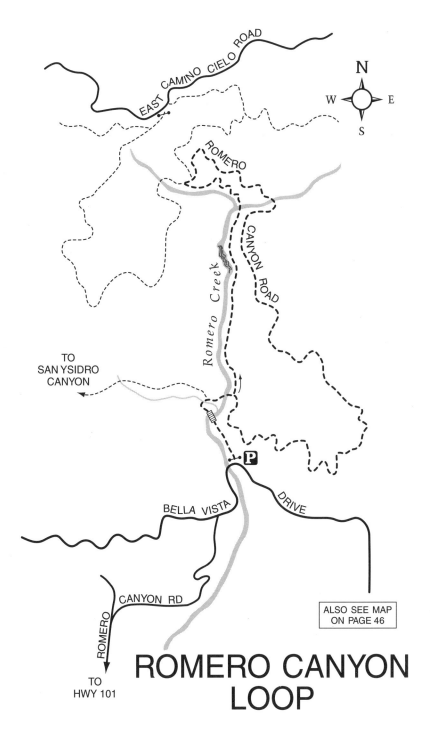

EAST CAMINO CIELO ROAD

N
W · E
S

ROMERO

CANYON ROAD

Romero Creek

TO
SAN YSIDRO
CANYON

P

BELLA VISTA DRIVE

CANYON RD

ROMERO

TO
HWY 101

ALSO SEE MAP
ON PAGE 46

ROMERO CANYON LOOP

Hike 28
Ennisbrook Trail

Hiking distance: 2.4 miles round trip
Hiking time: 1.4 hours
Elevation gain: Near level
Maps: U.S.G.S. Carpinteria
      Montecito Trails Foundation Trails Map

Summary of hike: The Ennisbrook Trail (also known as the San Ysidro Creekside Trail), in the heart of Montecito, meanders through an oak, olive and eucalyptus woodland. San Ysidro Creek flows through a 44-acre preserve under old stone bridges that span the creek.

Driving directions: From Santa Barbara, drive southbound on Highway 101 to Montecito, and exit on San Ysidro Road. Drive one block north to San Leandro Lane and turn right. Continue 0.7 miles to 1710 San Leandro Lane, and park alongside the road. En route to the trailhead, San Leandro Lane jogs to the left and back again to the right.

Hiking directions: From San Leandro Lane, hike north along the east bank of San Ysidro Creek for 100 yards to an old stone bridge crossing the creek. Instead of crossing, stay on the footpath to the right along the same side of the creek. At 0.4 miles, the trail joins Ennisbrook Drive for 100 yards before dropping back down to the forest and creek. Cross the stone bridge over San Ysidro Creek, continuing upstream to a junction. The left fork leads to a cul-de-sac at the south end of East Valley Lane. Bear to the right, crossing a stream through a lush, overgrown forest. At 1.2 miles is another signed junction. The left fork also leads to East Valley Lane. Take the right fork and cross San Ysidro Creek. Once across, the trail winds through a eucalyptus forest and ends a short distance ahead at private property. To return, reverse your route.

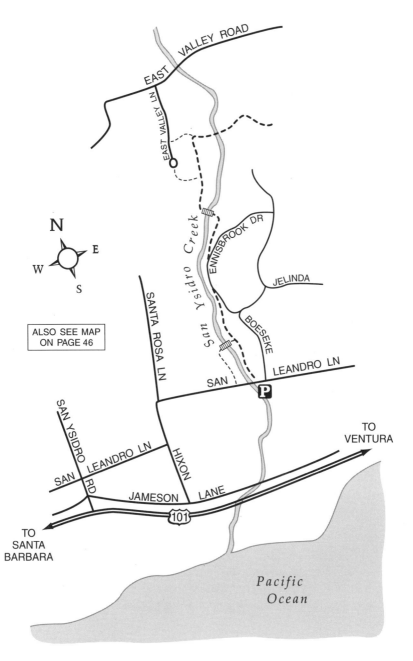

ENNISBROOK TRAIL

Hike 29
San Ysidro Canyon

Hiking distance: 3.7 miles round trip
Hiking time: 2 hours
Elevation gain: 1,200 feet
Maps: U.S.G.S. Carpinteria and Santa Barbara
Santa Barbara Front Country Recreational Map

Summary of hike: The San Ysidro Trail heads up the pictur-esque San Ysidro Canyon along the cascading San Ysidro Creek. The steep, narrow, upper canyon is filled with small waterfalls, continuous cascades and pools. This hike leads to San Ysidro Falls, a beautiful 60-foot waterfall.

Driving directions: From Santa Barbara, drive southbound on Highway 101 to Montecito, and exit on San Ysidro Road. Drive one mile north to East Valley Road and turn right. Continue 0.8 miles to Park Lane and turn left. Drive 0.3 miles to East Mountain Drive and bear to the left. The trailhead is 0.2 miles ahead on the right. Park along East Mountain Drive.

Hiking directions: The signed trail heads to the right (north), parallel to a wooden fence. Proceed on the tree covered lane past a few homes to a paved road. Follow the road 100 yards uphill to an unpaved road. Take the dirt road and drop into the cool and lush San Ysidro Canyon. At a half mile, there is a trail junction with the old Pueblo Trail on the right, ascending east. Soon after is the McMenemy Trail on the left (Hike 30). Continue up the canyon on the fire road past anoth-er gate and a large eroded sandstone wall on the left. A hun-dred yards beyond the rock wall, power lines cross high above the trail near another junction. Take the footpath bearing to the right, leaving the fire road. The trail gains elevation up the canyon past continuous cascades and pools. Several side paths lead to the left down to San Ysidro Creek. At 1.5 miles, a switchback and metal railing marks the beginning of the steep-er ascent up canyon. The trail crosses a stream at 1.8 miles. To the right is a short side scramble up the narrow canyon to various pools, falls and cascades. Back on the main trail, continue 100 yards to a trail fork. The right fork leads to the base of San Ysidro Falls. This is our turnaround spot.

To hike further, the left fork climbs out of the canyon to the Camino Cielo Ridge, gaining 1,800 feet in 2.5 miles.

EAST CAMINO CIELO ROAD

San Ysidro Falls

N

W   E

S

ALSO SEE MAP
ON PAGE 46

MONTECITO
PEAK
3,214'

San Ysidro Creek

Hot Springs Creek

CATWAY

TO
BUENA VISTA
TRAIL

TO
BUENA VISTA
TRAIL

EDISON

OLD PUEBLO TR.

30

McMENEMY TRAIL
McMENEMY
BENCH

LANE

PARK

P

EAST MOUNTAIN
DRIVE

SAN YSIDRO
CANYON

TO
HWY 101

Hike 30
McMenemy Trail

Hiking distance: 5.5 miles round trip
Hiking time: 3 hours
Elevation gain: 1,000 feet
Maps: U.S.G.S. Carpinteria and Santa Barbara
Santa Barbara Front Country Recreational Map

Summary of hike: The McMenemy Trail is a connector trail linking San Ysidro Canyon and Hot Springs Canyon. This hike begins in the picturesque San Ysidro Canyon. The trail crosses over the ridge between the canyons to meadows and scenic overlooks. It then descends into Hot Springs Canyon below Montecito Peak.

Driving directions: From Santa Barbara, drive southbound on Highway 101 to Montecito, and exit on San Ysidro Road. Drive one mile north to East Valley Road and turn right. Continue 0.8 miles to Park Lane and turn left. Drive 0.3 miles to East Mountain Drive and bear to the left. The trailhead is 0.2 miles ahead on the right. Park along East Mountain Drive.

Hiking directions: The signed trail heads to the right (north), parallel to a wooden fence. Proceed on the tree-covered lane past a few homes to a paved road. Follow the road 100 yards uphill to an unpaved road. Take the dirt road and drop into San Ysidro Canyon. At a half mile, there is a trail junction with the signed McMenemy Trail on the left. Go left, rock hopping across San Ysidro Creek into a eucalyptus woodland. Head up a short hill to another junction. Take the left fork up to a meadow overlooking the ocean. Switchbacks lead up to a trail split. Both trails lead up McMenemy Hill to a ridge with a rock bench on a 1,250-foot perch. There are first-class views up and down the coastline from McMenemy Bench. From the meadow, the Girard Trail heads north to the Edison Catway. Proceed downhill on the McMenemy Trail past a water tank and rock outcroppings. Cross a small stream near a waterfall, and head to a signed junction on a ridge. The right fork, Saddle Rock Trail, leads a short distance up to a garden of large sandstone boulders and onto the Edison Catway. This route can be combined with the Girard Trail, forming a loop back to McMenemy Bench. The left fork leads 0.2 miles down to the unpaved Hot Springs Road and Hot Springs Creek.

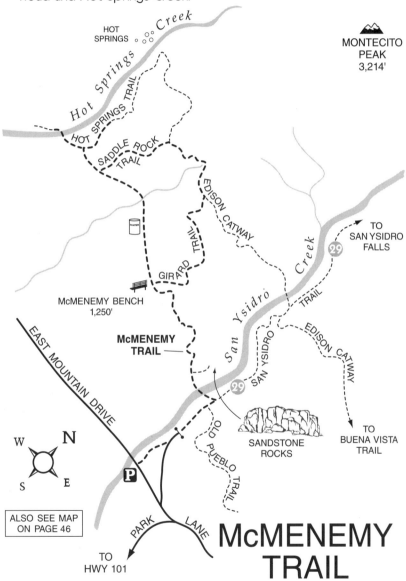

McMENEMY TRAIL

Hike 31
Hammonds Meadow Trail

Hiking distance: 2 miles round trip
Hiking time: 1 hour
Elevation gain: Level
Maps: U.S.G.S. Santa Barbara
       The Thomas Guide—Santa Barbara and Vicinity

Summary of hike: The Hammonds Meadow Trail strolls through a forest of palm and eucalyptus trees with tall, flowering bougainvillea bushes. The pastoral path connects three beaches between the Miramar and Biltmore Hotels. The walking path passes beautiful homes, crossing Montecito Creek to the beachfront.

Driving directions: From Santa Barbara, drive southbound on Highway 101 to Montecito, and exit on San Ysidro Road south. Turn right on Eucalyptus Lane, and drive south 0.1 mile to a small parking lot at the end of the road, just past Bonnymede Drive. If the lot is full, an additional parking area is on Humphrey Road, the first street north.

Hiking directions: The signed trail begins to the west. (A short detour straight ahead to the south leads down a few steps to coastal access at Miramar Beach.) Take the Hammonds Meadow Trail through a beautiful forested lane surrounded by every color of flowering bougainvillea. At 0.2 miles, a bridge crosses Montecito Creek. Along both sides of the creek are coastal access paths. Cross the bridge and parallel the west side of the creek to Hammonds Beach. Follow the shoreline to the west for a quarter mile, reaching the Biltmore Hotel at the east end of Butterfly Beach. Continue along the coastline west on Butterfly Beach below the bluff terrace. Several staircases lead up to Channel Drive. This is our turnaround spot. After beach combing, return along the same path.

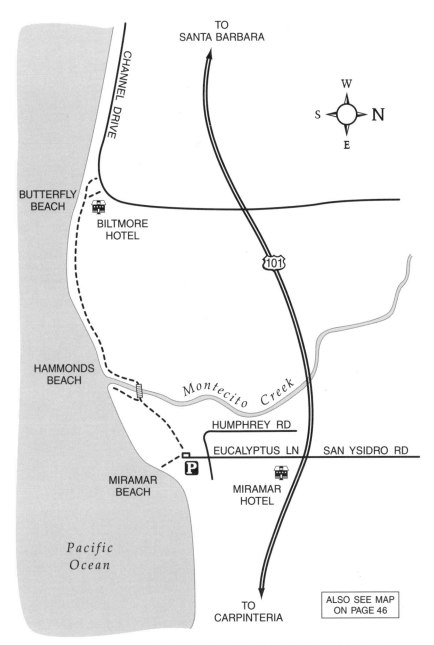

HAMMONDS MEADOW TRAIL

Hike 32
Cold Spring Canyon
East Fork to Montecito Overlook

Hiking distance: 3.2 miles round trip
Hiking time: 1.5 hours
Elevation gain: 900 feet
Maps: U.S.G.S. Santa Barbara
       Santa Barbara Front Country Recreational Map

Summary of hike: The hike up the East Fork of Cold Spring Canyon follows Cold Spring Creek through an alder, bay and oak forest. Between the steep canyon walls are creek crossings, deep pools and waterfalls. The trail leads to the Montecito Overlook, a spectacular vista point with a sweeping panorama of the mountains, ocean and the Channel Islands.

Driving directions: From Santa Barbara, drive southbound on Highway 101. Take the Hot Springs Road exit in Montecito and turn left. Drive 0.1 mile to Hot Springs Road and turn left again. Continue 2.2 miles to East Mountain Drive and turn left. Drive 1.1 mile to the Cold Spring trailhead on the right, located where the creek flows across the paved road. Park along the road.

Hiking directions: Access the trail from either side of Cold Spring Creek. Both trails join a short distance ahead on the east side of the creek. At a quarter mile is a bench, pool and junction with the West Fork Trail on the left (Hike 33). Continue north on the same side of the creek. The trail gains elevation up the canyon to a creek crossing at 0.6 miles. Rock hop across the creek, and continue uphill through the shady forest past waterfalls and pools to another creek crossing at 0.8 miles. After crossing, switchbacks lead up the mountainside away from the creek. At 1.3 miles, the trail joins a utility service road. Take the road a short distance to the right and up onto a knoll—Montecito Overlook. This is our turnaround spot.

To hike further, continue 100 yards east along the service

road to another junction with a trail veering off to the left. The trail leads two miles further to Montecito Peak, adding 1,550 feet to the hike.

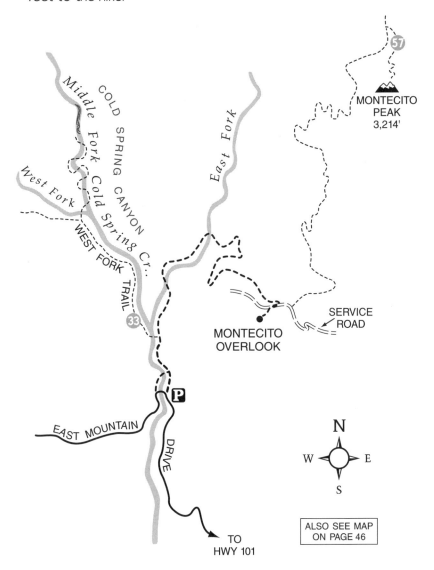

MONTECITO PEAK 3,214'

MONTECITO OVERLOOK

SERVICE ROAD

Middle Fork

COLD SPRING CANYON

West Fork

East Fork

Middle Fork Cold Spring Cr.

WEST FORK TRAIL

EAST MOUNTAIN

DRIVE

P

TO HWY 101

N
W E
S

ALSO SEE MAP ON PAGE 46

COLD SPRING CANYON
EAST FORK TO MONTECITO OVERLOOK

Hike 33
Cold Spring Canyon
West Fork to Tangerine Falls

Hiking distance: 3.5 miles round trip
Hiking time: 2 hours
Elevation gain: 900 feet
Maps: U.S.G.S. Santa Barbara
Santa Barbara Front Country Recreational Map

Summary of hike: This hike up Cold Spring Canyon passes sandstone formations, numerous cascades, pools and waterfalls as the trail parallels three creeks. The forested hike includes an off-trail scramble up a gorge to a 200-foot waterfall known as Tangerine Falls.

Driving directions: From Santa Barbara, drive southbound on Highway 101. Take the Hot Springs Road exit in Montecito and turn left. Drive 0.1 mile to Hot Springs Road and turn left again. Continue 2.2 miles to East Mountain Drive and turn left. Drive 1.1 mile to the Cold Spring trailhead on the right, where the creek flows across the paved road. Park along the road.

Hiking directions: Hike north along either side of Cold Spring Creek. Within minutes, both trails join on the east side of the creek. Proceed up canyon to a junction with the West Fork Cold Spring Trail on the left by a bench and small waterfall, located where two creeks merge. Cross the creek to the left, and head up the western wall of West Fork Canyon parallel to the creek. At 0.8 miles, an unsigned junction takes off to the right. Go to the right, leaving the main trail. Cross a seasonal creek and enter the Middle Fork of Cold Spring Canyon. This side trail follows the creek past pools and waterfalls as you work your way to the base of Tangerine Falls. This unmaintained trail is a scramble over boulders and old water pipes in a steep but beautiful canyon. Use caution!

To hike further, return to the main trail. Continue for one mile to Gibraltar Road, climbing 700 feet out of the canyon.

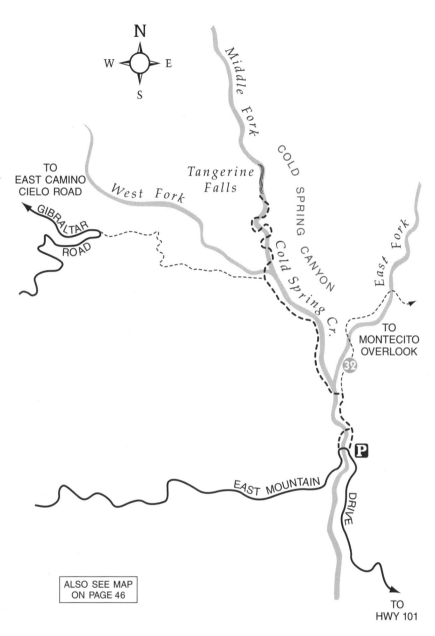

COLD SPRING CANYON
WEST FORK TO TANGERINE FALLS

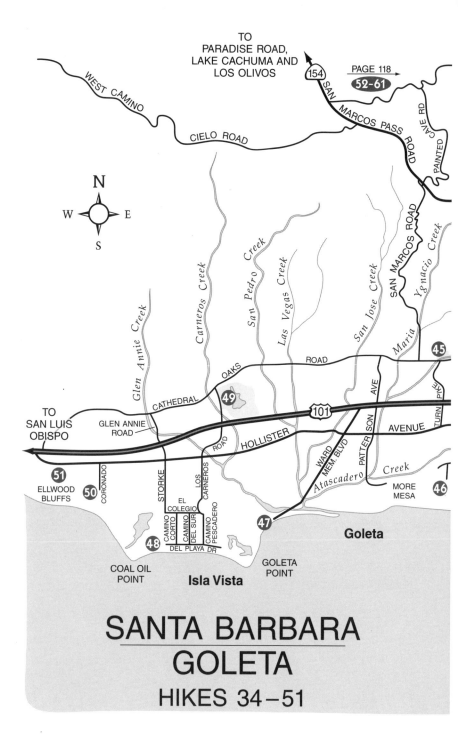

TO
PARADISE ROAD,
LAKE CACHUMA AND
LOS OLIVOS

154

PAGE 118
52-61

WEST CAMINO

CIELO ROAD

SAN MARCOS PASS ROAD

PAINTED CAVE RD

N
W E
S

Glen Annie Creek

Carneros Creek

San Pedro Creek

Las Vegas Creek

San Jose Creek

Ygnacio Creek

SAN MARCOS ROAD

Maria

45

ROAD

OAKS

49

CATHEDRAL

TO
SAN LUIS
OBISPO

GLEN ANNIE
ROAD

ROAD

HOLLISTER

AVE

101

PATTERSON

AVENUE

TURN PIKE

51

ELLWOOD
BLUFFS

50

CORONADO

STORKE

EL
COLEGIO

LOS CARNEROS

WARD MEM. BLVD

Atascadero

Creek

MORE
MESA

46

48

CAMINO CORTO

CAMINO DEL SUR

CAMINO PESCADERO

DEL PLAYA DR

47

Goleta

COAL OIL
POINT

Isla Vista

GOLETA
POINT

SANTA BARBARA
GOLETA
HIKES 34–51

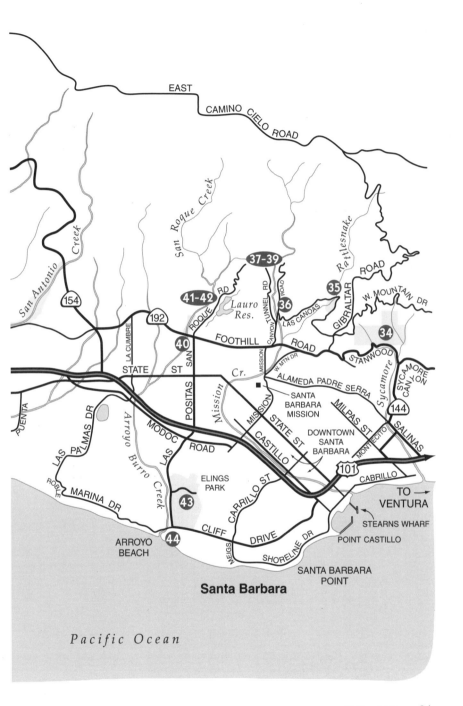

EAST CAMINO CIELO ROAD

San Rogue Creek

San Antonio Creek

Rattlesnake

37-39

41-42

35

GIBRALTAR ROAD

W. MOUNTAIN DR

154

RD

Lauro Res.

CANYON TUNNEL RD

ROAD

36

LAS CANOAS

34

192

STANWOOD

POSITAS

SAN ROQUE

40

FOOTHILL ROAD

W. MTN DR

Sycamore

SYCAMORE CAN

LA CUMBRE

STATE ST

Cr.

Mission

ALAMEDA PADRE SERRA

144

SANTA BARBARA MISSION

MISSION ST

STATE ST

CASTILLO

MILPAS ST

SALINAS

PUENTA

LAS PALMAS DR

Arroyo Burro Creek

MODOC ROAD

LAS POSITAS

DOWNTOWN SANTA BARBARA

MONTECITO

101

CABRILLO

TO → VENTURA

LAS ROBLE

MARINA DR

ELINGS PARK

CARRILLO ST

STEARNS WHARF

43

CLIFF DRIVE

SHORELINE DR

POINT CASTILLO

ARROYO BEACH

44

NEIGS

SANTA BARBARA POINT

Santa Barbara

Pacific Ocean

Hike 34
Parma Park

Hiking distance: 2.5 mile loop
Hiking time: 1.4 hours
Elevation gain: 300 feet
Maps: U.S.G.S. Santa Barbara
   The Thomas Guide—Santa Barbara & Vicinity

Summary of hike: Parma Park is a wonderful, undeveloped park on more than 200 acres in the foothills of Sycamore Canyon. Coyote Creek, Sycamore Creek and several seasonal streams flow through the park. Some of the hiking and equestrian trails follow the lush, forested canyon with old growth trees. Others lead to grassy knolls overlooking the surrounding hills. The trails in the park are intentionally unmarked.

Driving directions: In Santa Barbara, take Sycamore Canyon Road north to Stanwood Drive and turn left. Drive 0.7 miles to Parma Park on the right. The parking lot gate is usually locked. Park across the road in the parking pullouts.

Hiking directions: Hike north past the entrance sign and gate, crossing an old stone bridge. At the end of the paved road is an open picnic area and a 4-way junction. To the right, the unmarked Rowe Trail leads downhill and across a branch of Sycamore Creek. Continue on this trail to the ridge above Stanwood Drive. Head east along the ridge, parallel to the road below. At the east end, the trail curves left to the Parma Fire Road on a knoll overlooking Sycamore Canyon, the Santa Ynez Mountains and the ocean. Head left, returning along the fire road. The trail descends to a series of knolls and into an oak woodland in the canyon. Cross Sycamore Creek and complete the loop.

A second hiking trail heads north from the 4-way junction. The trail crisscrosses Sycamore Creek up a forested canyon. At 0.3 miles, the trail leaves the creek and switchbacks up to the ridge at Mountain Drive. Return along the same route.

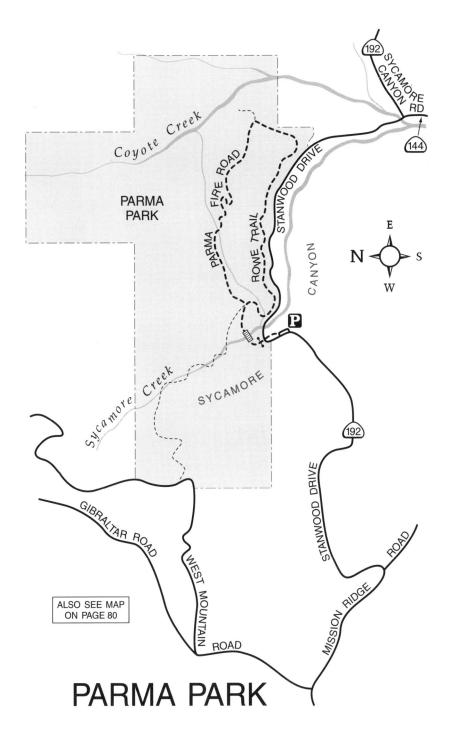

192

SYCAMORE CANYON RD

144

Coyote Creek

PARMA PARK

PARMA FIRE ROAD

ROWE TRAIL

STANWOOD DRIVE

CANYON

E
N — S
W

P

SYCAMORE

Sycamore Creek

SYCAMORE

192

STANWOOD DRIVE

GIBRALTAR ROAD

WEST MOUNTAIN ROAD

MISSION RIDGE ROAD

ALSO SEE MAP
ON PAGE 80

PARMA PARK

Hike 35
Rattlesnake Canyon

Hiking distance: 3.5 miles round trip
Hiking time: 2 hours
Elevation gain: 1,000 feet
Maps: U.S.G.S. Santa Barbara
Santa Barbara Front Country Recreational Map

Summary of hike: Rattlesnake Canyon is one of Santa Barbara's most popular trails. The trail leads up the winding canyon through a lush, riparian forest with many pools, small waterfalls, and stream crossings. There is a grotto, meadow and a panoramic vista overlooking the Pacific Ocean and the Channel Islands. Rattlesnake Canyon received its name for its winding canyon, not for snake occupancy.

Driving directions: From the Santa Barbara Mission, take Mission Canyon Road north towards the mountains for 0.6 miles to Foothill Road—turn right. Drive 0.2 miles to Mission Canyon Road and turn left. Continue 0.5 miles to Las Conoas Road and turn sharply to the right, following the Skofield Park sign. Take this winding road 1.2 miles to the trailhead, located by a beautiful stone bridge over Rattlesnake Creek. Park in the pullouts along the right side of the road or a short distance ahead in Skofield Park.

Hiking directions: Head north past the trail sign along the west side of the stone bridge. Rock hop across the creek to a wide trail. Head to the left another half mile to a trail split. Continue straight ahead on the narrower trail, staying in the canyon and creek. Descend to the cascading Rattlesnake Creek and recross to the west side of the creek. The trail climbs out of the canyon via switchbacks. At 1.3 miles is the first of two successive creek crossings. Between these crossings are cascades, small waterfalls, pools, flat sunbathing boulders and a rock grotto. Back on the west side of the watercourse, the trail climbs to Tin Can Flat, a large, grassy meadow with views of the surrounding mountains. Just beyond the meadow is a junction with the Rattlesnake Canyon—Tunnel Connector Trail. This is the turnaround spot. Return along the same path.

To hike further, take the right fork uphill to the east for 0.7 miles to Gibraltar Road, or take the left fork uphill to the west 0.8 miles to the Tunnel Trail in Mission Canyon (Hike 38).

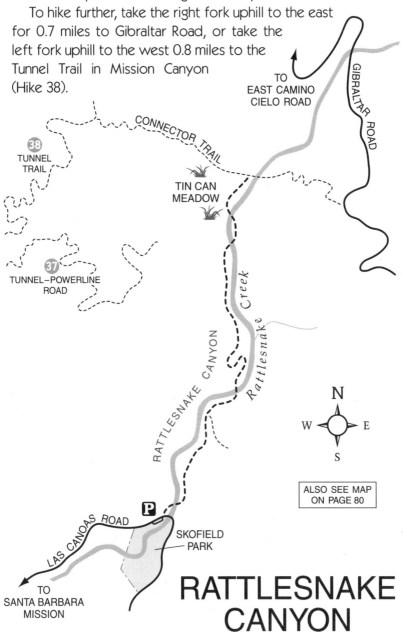

RATTLESNAKE
CANYON

Hike 36
Santa Barbara Botanic Garden

Hiking distance: 2 miles round trip
Hiking time: 2 hours
Elevation gain: 50 feet
Maps: Santa Barbara Botanic Garden Visitors Map
      Guide to the Santa Barbara Botanic Garden

Summary of hike: The Santa Barbara Botanic Garden has seven looping nature trails totaling 5.5 miles. The trails cover a wide variety of habitats on the 65-acre grounds. Through the heart of the garden flows Mission Creek. The trails pass through a canyon, a redwood forest, over bridges, past a waterfall and across a historic dam built in 1906. This hike is only a suggested route. Many other paths can be chosen to view areas of your own interests.

Driving directions: From the Santa Barbara Mission, take Mission Canyon Road north towards the mountains for 0.6 miles to Foothill Road—turn right. Drive 0.2 miles to Mission Canyon Road and turn left. Continue 0.9 miles to the botanic garden parking lot on the left at 1212 Mission Canyon Road.

Hiking directions: From the entrance, head to the right past a pond and through a meadow. Past the meadow is the Redwood Forest. (The Woodland Trail is a side loop to the east.) The trail leads downhill towards Mission Creek before looping back to the south under the forested canopy. Cross Mission Dam and continue parallel to the creek. (The Pritchett Trail is a hillside loop to the west.) Campbell Bridge crosses the creek to the left, returning to the entrance. For a longer hike, continue south to the island section. The Easton–Aqueduct Trail loops around the hillside and descends to the creek at Stone Creek Crossing. Once across, head up the rock steps into the Manzanita Section, and return to the garden entrance.

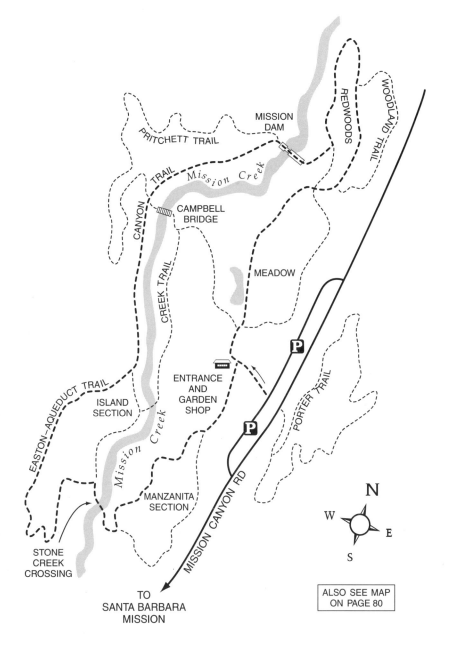

MISSION DAM

PRITCHETT TRAIL

REDWOODS

WOODLAND TRAIL

CANYON TRAIL

Mission Creek

CAMPBELL BRIDGE

CREEK TRAIL

MEADOW

EASTON–AQUEDUCT TRAIL

ISLAND SECTION

Mission Creek

ENTRANCE AND GARDEN SHOP

P

P

PORTER TRAIL

MANZANITA SECTION

STONE CREEK CROSSING

MISSION CANYON RD

TO SANTA BARBARA MISSION

N

W

E

S

ALSO SEE MAP ON PAGE 80

SANTA BARBARA
BOTANIC GARDEN

Hike 37
Tunnel—Powerline Road

Hiking distance: 5.6 miles round trip
Hiking time: 2.5 hours
Elevation gain: 1,300 feet
Maps: U.S.G.S. Santa Barbara
Santa Barbara Front Country Recreational Map

Summary of hike: The Tunnel-Powerline Road is a utility easement road sometimes referred to as the Edison Catwalk. The trail is a steady, but not steep, uphill climb following the contours of the hillside. The hike leads to a hilltop overlook of Rattlesnake Canyon and offers great views of Santa Barbara, the coastline and the Channel Islands.

Driving directions: From the Santa Barbara Mission, take Mission Canyon Road north towards the mountains for 0.6 miles to Foothill Road—turn right. Drive 0.2 miles to Mission Canyon Road and turn left. Continue 0.3 miles and bear left at a road split onto Tunnel Road. Drive 1.1 mile and park along the right side of the road near the road's end.

Hiking directions: Hike to the end of Tunnel Road and past the gate. Head uphill, winding around the hillside with great views below of the city and ocean. At 0.7 miles, the trail crosses a bridge over Mission Creek and Little Fern Canyon Falls (cover photo). Arrive at a trail split where the paved trail ends. Bear to the right, staying on the unpaved road as it gains elevation along the contours of the hills. At 1.4 miles, there is a junction on the left with a connector trail to the Tunnel Trail (Hike 38). Stay to the right, entering a shady, forested area. The grade gets steeper as you near the top. The trail ends on the hilltop by utility poles overlooking Rattlesnake Canyon (Hike 35). To return, reverse your route.

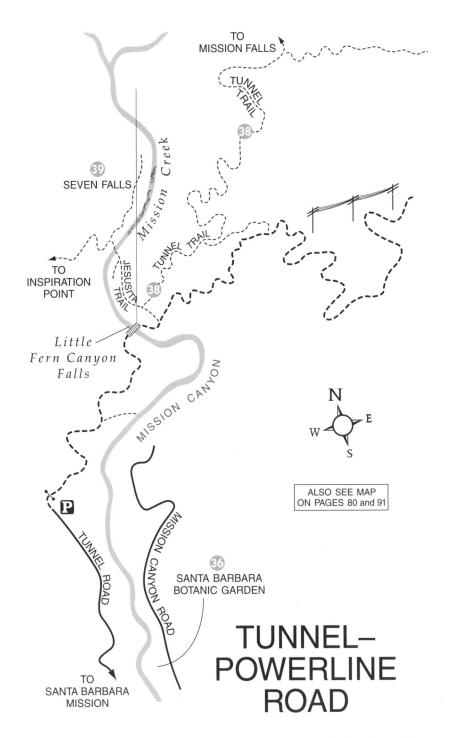

TO
MISSION FALLS

TUNNEL
TRAIL

38

Mission Creek

39
SEVEN FALLS

TUNNEL TRAIL

TO
INSPIRATION
POINT

JESUSITA
TRAIL

38

Little
Fern Canyon
Falls

MISSION CANYON

N
W · E
S

ALSO SEE MAP
ON PAGES 80 and 91

P

TUNNEL ROAD

MISSION CANYON ROAD

36
SANTA BARBARA
BOTANIC GARDEN

TO
SANTA BARBARA
MISSION

TUNNEL–
POWERLINE
ROAD

Hike 38
Tunnel Trail to Mission Falls

Hiking distance: 5.8 miles round trip
Hiking time: 3 hours
Elevation gain: 1,800 feet
Maps: U.S.G.S. Santa Barbara
    Santa Barbara Front Country Recreational Map

Summary of hike: The Tunnel Trail is named for a diversion tunnel built at the turn of the century that brings fresh water to Santa Barbara. The hike passes beautiful, weathered sandstone outcroppings on the way to panoramic views of Santa Barbara and the Channel Islands. The Tunnel Trail climbs along the eastern wall of Mission Canyon to an overlook atop the 200-foot Mission Falls.

Driving directions: To arrive at the trailhead, follow the driving directions for Hike 37.

Hiking directions: Head up Tunnel Road and past the trailhead gate. Continue up the curving road past Mission Creek. A bridge crosses the creek over Little Fern Canyon Falls (cover photo). At 0.7 miles, the paved road ends at a three-way junction. Bear left on the Jesusita Trail for 150 yards to the Tunnel Trail junction on the right. Take this footpath through the brush to a junction with a connector trail at 1.2 miles. Cross the road, picking up the trail again. The steady, uphill trail passes the signed Rattlesnake Canyon—Tunnel Connector Trail at 2.3 miles on the right—stay left. Mission Falls can be seen across the canyon just before reaching this junction. Continue 0.7 miles to the creek crossing above the falls. It is a difficult scramble to see the falls up close, but you will be able to sit among the large sandstone boulders above the falls and marvel at the views. Return along the same route.

To continue hiking, it is 1.2 miles further to East Camino Cielo Road.

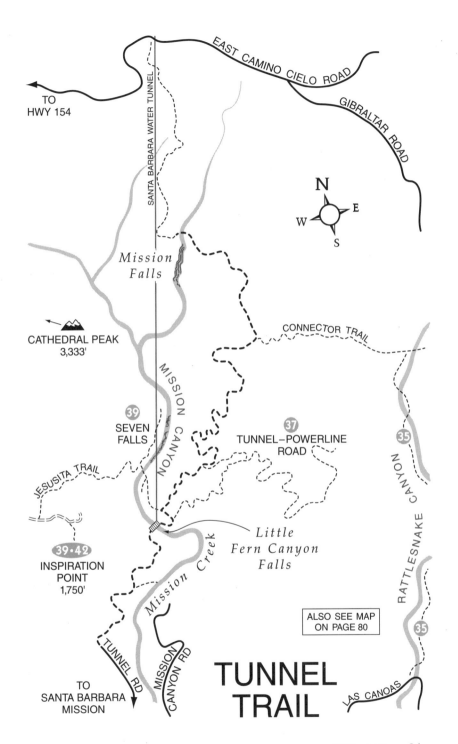

EAST CAMINO CIELO ROAD

GIBRALTAR ROAD

TO
HWY 154

SANTA BARBARA WATER TUNNEL

N
W   E
S

Mission Falls

CATHEDRAL PEAK
3,333'

CONNECTOR TRAIL

MISSION CANYON

39
SEVEN
FALLS

37
TUNNEL–POWERLINE
ROAD

35

JESUSITA TRAIL

39·42
INSPIRATION
POINT
1,750'

Mission Creek

Little Fern Canyon Falls

RATTLESNAKE CANYON

ALSO SEE MAP
ON PAGE 80

35

TUNNEL RD

MISSION CANYON RD

TO
SANTA BARBARA
MISSION

LAS CANOAS

TUNNEL TRAIL

Hike 39
Seven Falls and Inspiration Point

Hiking distance: 3.7 miles round trip
Hiking time: 2.5 hours
Elevation gain: 800 feet
Maps: U.S.G.S. Santa Barbara
        Santa Barbara Front Country Recreational Map

Summary of hike: Seven Falls is in a beautiful, sculpted gorge in Mission Canyon. Mission Creek cascades down the canyon and over boulders, creating more than a dozen waterfalls. The waterfalls drop into bowls etched into the sandstone rock, forming deep, rock-rimmed pools. One mile beyond Seven Falls is Inspiration Point, a 1,750-foot scenic overlook with sweeping vistas of the Pacific Ocean, the Channel Islands, Santa Barbara and Goleta.

Driving directions: To arrive at the trailhead, follow the driving directions for Hike 37.

Hiking directions: Follow the hiking directions for Hike 38 to the trail split at 0.7 miles. At the three-way junction, where the pavement ends, the right fork is a powerline access road (Hike 37). Take the left fork—the Jesusita Trail—into Mission Canyon. The trail descends into the forest to Mission Creek. Once across the creek, leave the Jesusita Trail, which leads to Inspiration Point. Instead, take the narrow path to the right up the west side of the canyon and parallel to the creek. Be careful! This is an unmaintained trail and can be very tricky. Boulder climbing and branch dodging is involved as you slowly work your way up the narrow gorge past an endless display of waterfalls, cascades and pools. Choose you own swimming hole and turnaround spot. There are additional waterfalls and pools down canyon from the main trail.

To continue to Inspiration Point, follow the main Jesusita Trail from Mission Creek. The trail switchbacks one mile up the chaparral covered canyon wall past sandstone outcroppings. At the summit is a T-junction with a power line service road. Cross the road and curve right to the south edge of the ridge to an inspirational point, but not *the* Inspiration Point. Return to the power pole road, and walk a short distance east. Watch for a footpath on the right leading into the brush. This narrow path ends 300 yards ahead at Inspiration Point on a jumble of sandstone boulders directly below Cathedral Peak. Return along the same route. The Jesusita Trail continues west into San Roque Canyon (Hike 42).

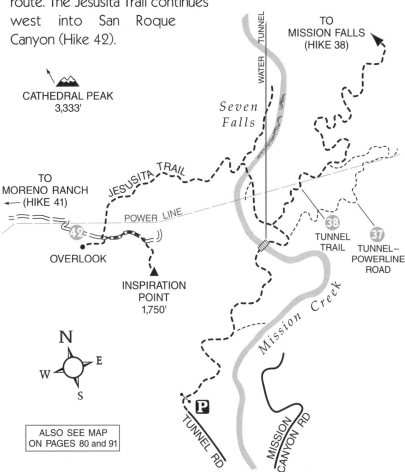

SEVEN FALLS
INSPIRATION POINT

Hike 40
Stevens Park

Hiking distance: 1.8 miles round trip
Hiking time: 1 hour
Elevation gain: 150 feet
Maps: U.S.G.S. Santa Barbara

Summary of hike: Stevens Park is a beautiful oak-shaded park at the bottom of San Roque Canyon. San Roque Creek flows down the forested canyon through the length of Stevens Park. An easy creekside nature trail winds through the park past bedrock mortars, ancient holes worn into the rock by Chumash Indians from grinding acorns into meal. The trail continues from the north end of the park to the Jesusita Trail, connecting San Roque Canyon with Mission Canyon.

Driving directions: From Highway 101 in Santa Barbara, exit on Las Positas Road. Drive 1.2 miles north to Calle Fresno on the left. (Las Positas becomes San Roque after crossing State Street.) Turn left one block to Canon Drive. Turn right and quickly turn right again into the posted park entrance. Park in the spaces 0.1 mile ahead.

Hiking directions: Walk to the upper (north) end of the park and take the footpath along the east side of San Roque Creek. Enter the shady woodland and cross under the towering Foothill Road bridge. Pass through an oak and sycamore grove to an open grassy meadow on the right with views of Cathedral Peak. At the trail split, the right fork curves around the meadow and up the hill to San Roque Road, just north of Foothill Road. Go left and follow San Roque Creek upstream, passing a sandstone rock on the right with five bedrock mortars. Descend and cross the creek to an oak glen and a circle of large boulders overlooking the creek. Leave the creek and curve up the hillside. Cross over the ridge and continue to a second ridge at a concrete spillway outside the park boundary. Cross the spillway and follow the wide path along the left (west) side of the creek. Curve right and drop down to the banks of the creek again. Cross the creek, picking up the trail upstream. Climb the hill to a T-junction with the Jesusita Trail. The right fork leads 140 yards to San Roque Road. The left fork continues to Moreno Ranch and Inspiration Point (Hikes 41 and 42). Return to Stevens Park along the same route or hike a loop, returning on San Roque Road and Calle Fresno.

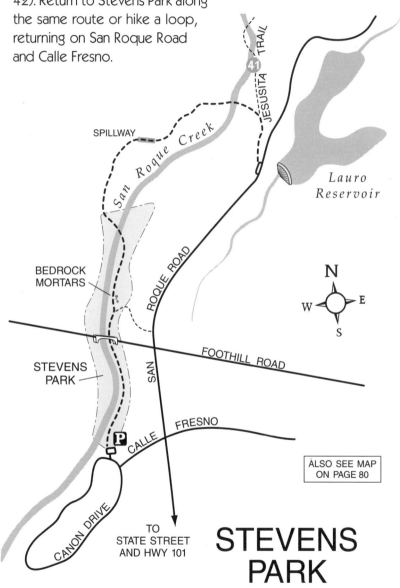

ALSO SEE MAP
ON PAGE 80

STEVENS
PARK

Hike 41
Jesusita Trail to Moreno Ranch

Hiking distance: 2.5 miles round trip
Hiking time: 1.5 hours
Elevation gain: 700 feet
Maps: U.S.G.S. Santa Barbara
       Santa Barbara Front Country Recreational Map

Summary of hike: The Jesusita Trail is a 4.5-mile trail that connects San Roque Canyon to Mission Canyon. This hike starts at Lauro Reservoir and heads up lower San Roque Canyon, parallel to a tributary of San Roque Creek. The trail winds through open grassy meadows and lush riparian habitat, with numerous creek crossings under the shade of oaks, sycamores, cottonwoods and willows.

Driving directions: From Highway 101 in Santa Barbara, exit on Las Positas Road. Drive 2 miles north to the posted trailhead parking area on the left, just beyond the filtration plant. (Las Positas Road becomes San Roque Road after crossing State Street.)

Hiking directions: Take the posted trail downhill into San Roque Canyon. Pass a junction on the left leading to Stevens Park (Hike 40). Traverse the east canyon wall above San Roque Creek. Descend and rock hop over the creek a couple of times. Follow the lazy watercourse upstream, winding through a shaded grove of twisted oaks to a signed Y-fork at a half mile. To the left is the Arroyo Burro Trail. Curve right, staying on the Jesusita Trail, and ascend a small hill, emerging from the forest to a large open meadow. Pass through the grassy plateau, and descend back into the forest to the creek. Cross to the west side of the creek by a pool at one mile. Cross the creek three more times in quick succession, reaching the Moreno Ranch entrance at a private, unpaved road. This is the end of the lower canyon and our turnaround spot. To hike further, continue with Hike 42 to Inspiration Point.

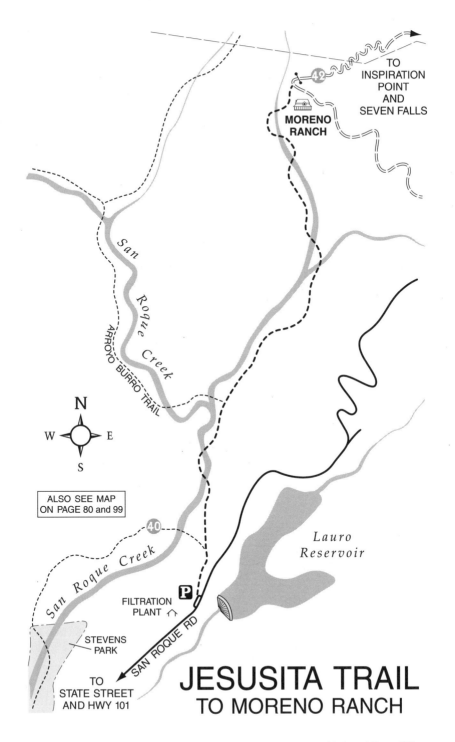

TO
INSPIRATION
POINT
AND
SEVEN FALLS

42

MORENO
RANCH

San

Roque

Creek

ARROYO BURRO TRAIL

N
W · E
S

ALSO SEE MAP
ON PAGE 80 and 99

40

San Roque Creek

Lauro
Reservoir

P

FILTRATION
PLANT

SAN ROQUE RD

STEVENS
PARK

TO
STATE STREET
AND HWY 101

JESUSITA TRAIL
TO MORENO RANCH

Hike 42
Jesusita Trail to Inspiration Point

Hiking distance: 6 miles round trip
Hiking time: 3 hours
Elevation gain: 1,300 feet
Maps: U.S.G.S. Santa Barbara

Summary of hike: Inspiration Point overlooks Santa Barbara, Goleta, the Pacific Ocean and the Channel Islands from a 1,750-foot perch below Cathedral Peak. The Jesusita Trail, connecting San Roque Canyon with Mission Canyon, crosses a ridge at Inspiration Point. This hike climbs stream-fed San Roque Canyon through the shaded woodland and traverses the front range to Inspiration Point.

Driving directions: From Highway 101 in Santa Barbara, exit on Las Positas Road. Drive 2 miles north to the posted trailhead parking area on the left, just beyond the filtration plant. (Las Positas Road becomes San Roque Road after crossing State Street.)

Hiking directions: Follow the hiking directions to the Moreno Ranch entrance—Hike 41. Walk up the unpaved road 50 yards and curve right, following the trail sign. Pass through a trail gate, and continue to the east on the unpaved road. Cross a stream and pick up the posted footpath on the left. Traverse the north slope of the rock-walled canyon. Cross over to the south canyon wall and climb a series of 12 switchbacks out of the canyon to a magnificent vista of Santa Barbara and the coastline. Head east through the chaparral, zigzagging up the mountain while overlooking the city and ocean. Pass large sculpted sandstone formations on the right, and cross under power lines to the ridge at a junction with the power pole road. Bear left 50 yards along the road to footpaths on both the left and right. To the left, the Jesusita Trail descends from the ridge into Mission Canyon to Seven Falls (Hike 39). The right path curves along the south edge of the ridge to what many believe is Inspiration Point, and is certainly inspirational. After resting and savoring the views, return to the power pole road. A short distance east, the road begins dropping slightly. Watch for a narrow footpath on the right that leads into the chaparral. Take the side path 300 yards to the actual Inspiration Point, located at a jumble of sandstone boulders directly beneath Cathedral Peak.

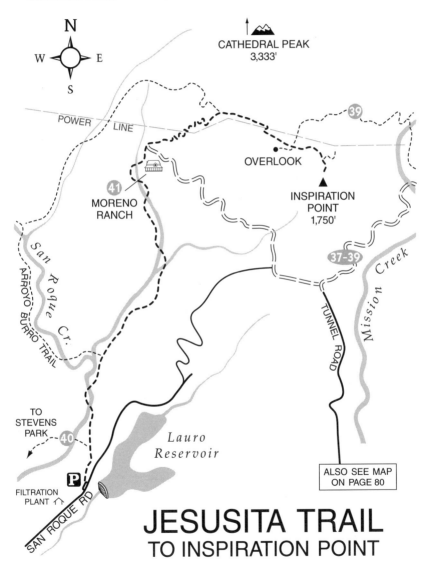

JESUSITA TRAIL
TO INSPIRATION POINT

Hike 43
Elings Park
The Sierra Club Trail

Hiking distance: 1.3 mile loop
Hiking time: 40 minutes
Elevation gain: 300 feet
Maps: U.S.G.S. Santa Barbara
The Thomas Guide—Santa Barbara & Vicinity

Summary of hike: Elings Park (formerly Las Positas Friendship Park) is a 236-acre hilltop park with a developed north side that includes baseball and soccer fields, gazebos, picnic areas, a war memorial and an amphitheater. The natural south side of the park has nature trails leading up to a ridge overlooking Santa Barbara with 360-degree views of the ocean harbor, the Channel Islands and the Santa Ynez Mountains.

Driving directions: From Highway 101 in Santa Barbara, exit on Las Positas Road. Drive 1.2 miles south (toward the ocean) to the Elings Park entrance on the left at 1298 Las Positas Road. Take the park road—Jerry Harwin Parkway—0.4 miles to the signed trailhead on the right across from the soccer fields. Park in the lots on the left or straight ahead.

Hiking directions: Cross the park road to the signed trailhead and a junction. Take the right fork up a series of switchbacks. Various side paths may be confusing, but all the trails lead up to the hilltop perch overlooking South Park and Jesuit Hill. At the top, the 360-degree views are stunning. The Sierra Club Trail follows the ridge to the east before sharply curving back to the west. This begins the winding descent, completing the loop back at the trailhead. A steep, direct route leads down the center of the hill between the switchbacks.

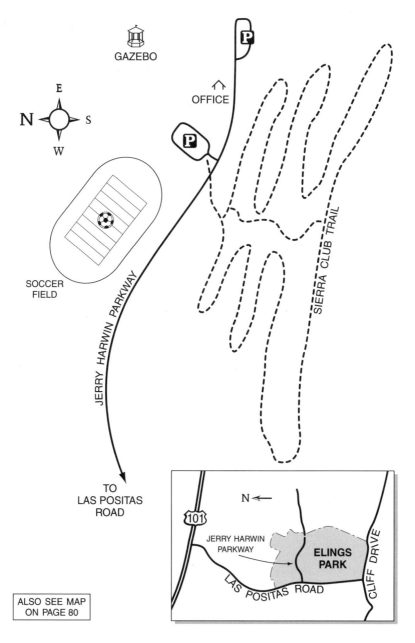

GAZEBO

E
N — S
W

OFFICE

P

P

SOCCER
FIELD

JERRY HARWIN PARKWAY

SIERRA CLUB TRAIL

TO
LAS POSITAS
ROAD

N ←

101

JERRY HARWIN
PARKWAY

ELINGS
PARK

CLIFF DRIVE

LAS POSITAS ROAD

ALSO SEE MAP
ON PAGE 80

ELINGS PARK

Hike 44
Douglas Family Preserve

Hiking distance: 1.5 miles round trip
Hiking time: 1 hour
Elevation gain: 150 feet
Maps: U.S.G.S. Santa Barbara
      The Thomas Guide—Santa Barbara & Vicinity

Summary of hike: The Douglas Family Preserve (also known as the Santa Barbara Coastal Bluffs) is a 70-acre grassy mesa with over 2,200 feet of rare, undeveloped ocean frontage. The preserve is covered with mature oak, eucalyptus and cypress trees. The trail loops around the 150-foot mesa along the edge of the cliffs. Below the cliffs is the picturesque Arroyo Burro Beach, locally known as Hendry's Beach. There are picnic areas and a paved biking and walking path.

Driving directions: From Highway 101 in Santa Barbara, exit on Las Positas Road. Head 1.8 miles south (towards the ocean) to Cliff Drive and turn right. Continue 0.2 miles to the Arroyo Burro Beach parking lot on the left and park.

Hiking directions: From the parking lot, walk east on Cliff Drive to Las Positas Road. From here, a trail heads south past a chained gate into the forest. The trail curves left through the shady canopy and up the hill. At the top, the trail levels out. Continue south along the eastern edge of the open space. Along the way, several paths intersect from the right and several access trails come in from the left. At the bluffs overlooking the ocean, head west along the cliffs. At the west end of the cliffs is an overlook of Arroyo Burro Beach. The trail curves to the right and loops back to a junction at the top of the hill. Head left, retracing your steps down the hill and back to the parking lot.

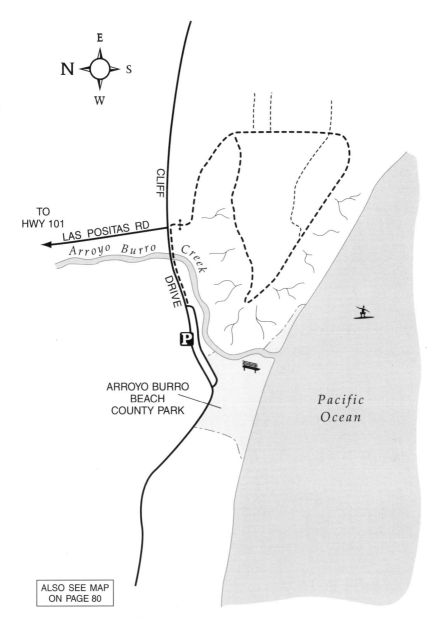

N E S W

TO
HWY 101

LAS POSITAS RD

Arroyo Burro Creek

CLIFF

DRIVE

P

ARROYO BURRO
BEACH
COUNTY PARK

Pacific
Ocean

ALSO SEE MAP
ON PAGE 80

DOUGLAS FAMILY
PRESERVE

Hike 45
San Antonio Creek Trail

Hiking distance: 3.4 miles round trip
Hiking time: 1.5 hours
Elevation gain: 200 feet
Maps: U.S.G.S. Goleta
          Santa Barbara Front Country Recreational Map

Summary of hike: The San Antonio Creek Trail follows the length of Tuckers Grove County Park in Goleta. The level trail travels through San Antonio Canyon along the watercourse of the creek past grassy meadows and a shady woodland of bay laurel, oak and sycamore trees.

Driving directions: From Santa Barbara, drive northbound on Highway 101, and exit on Turnpike Road in Goleta. Drive 0.6 miles north to Cathedral Oaks Road. Drive straight, through the intersection, entering Tuckers Grove Park. Bear to the right through the parking lot, and drive 0.3 miles to the last parking area.

Hiking directions: From the parking lot, hike up the road and past the upper picnic ground, Kiwanis Meadow. Cross through the opening in the log fence to the left, heading towards the creek. Take the trail upstream along the east side of San Antonio Creek. Numerous spur trails lead down to the creek. At one mile, rock hop across the creek, and continue to a second crossing located between steep canyon walls. After crossing, the trail ascends a hill to a bench near a concrete flood-control dam. Head left across the top of the dam. The trail proceeds to the right (upstream) and recrosses San Antonio Creek. The forested canyon trail passes alongside a chainlink fence on the east side of the stream. The trail ends at 1.7 miles under a bridge where the trail intersects with Highway 154. Return along the same trail.

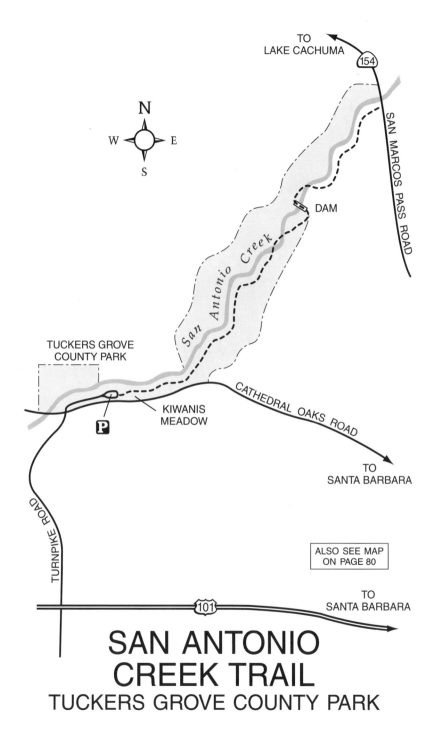

TO
LAKE CACHUMA

154

SAN MARCOS PASS ROAD

DAM

San Antonio Creek

TUCKERS GROVE
COUNTY PARK

CATHEDRAL OAKS ROAD

KIWANIS
MEADOW

P

TO
SANTA BARBARA

TURNPIKE ROAD

ALSO SEE MAP
ON PAGE 80

TO
SANTA BARBARA

101

SAN ANTONIO
CREEK TRAIL
TUCKERS GROVE COUNTY PARK

Hike 46
More Mesa

Hiking distance: 2.6 miles round trip
Hiking time: 1.5 hours
Elevation gain: Near level
Maps: U.S.G.S. Goleta
        The Thomas Guide—Santa Barbara and Vicinity

Summary of hike: More Mesa is an undeveloped 300-acre oceanfront expanse in Goleta. The flat blufftop mesa is marbled with hiking trails. The main trail follows the edge of the bluffs 120 feet above the ocean. The panoramic views extend from the Santa Ynez Mountains to the Channel Islands. The secluded, mile-long beach at the base of the mesa is clothing optional.

Driving directions: From Santa Barbara, drive northbound on Highway 101, and exit on Turnpike Road in Goleta. Turn left and drive 0.4 miles to Hollister Avenue. Turn left and go 0.3 miles to the first signal at Puente Drive. Turn right and continue 0.7 miles to Mockingbird Lane. (Along the way Puente Drive becomes Vieja Drive.) Parking is not allowed on Mockingbird Lane, so park on Vieja Drive by Mockingbird Lane.

    To access More Mesa from the west end, take Highway 101 to Patterson Avenue, and drive south 1.3 miles to the trailhead.

Hiking directions: Walk up Mockingbird Lane to the hiking path at the end of the street. Pass the metal trailhead gate, and cross the wide, flat marine terrace towards the ocean. At 0.6 miles, the path reaches a grove of mature eucalyptus trees lining the edge of the cliffs 120 feet above the ocean. A steep, narrow path descends down the cliffs to the secluded sandy beach. The left fork leads a short distance to a fenced residential area. Take the right fork, following the edge of the bluffs to the west. At 1.3 miles, the trail crosses a fenceline and ends by oceanfront homes. Various interconnecting trails crisscross the open space. Return along the same route for the best views.

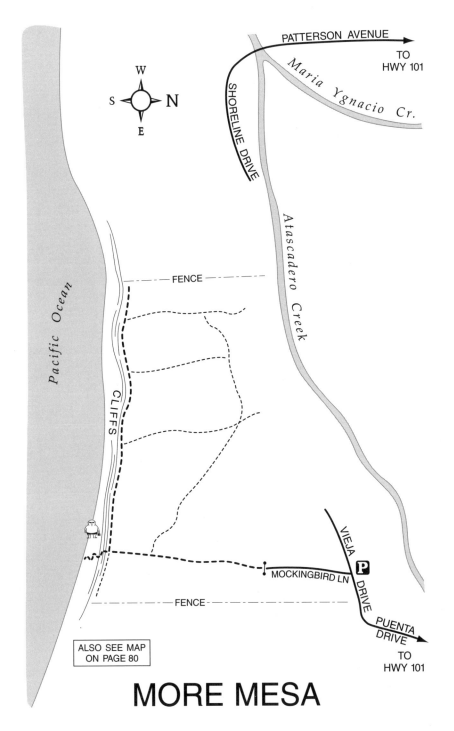

PATTERSON AVENUE

TO
HWY 101

Maria Ygnacio Cr.

SHORELINE DRIVE

Atascadero Creek

W
S — N
E

Pacific Ocean

FENCE

CLIFFS

FENCE

VIEJA DRIVE

P

MOCKINGBIRD LN

PUENTA DRIVE

TO
HWY 101

ALSO SEE MAP
ON PAGE 80

MORE MESA

Hike 47
Goleta Beach and the UCSB Lagoon

Hiking distance: 4 miles round trip
Hiking time: 2 hours
Elevation gain: 50 feet
Maps: U.S.G.S. Goleta
       The Thomas Guide—Santa Barbara & Vicinity

Summary of hike: This trail begins at Goleta Beach County Park and follows the coastal cliffs into the University of California—Santa Barbara. The trail circles the UCSB Lagoon to Goleta Point (also called Campus Point). The ocean surrounds the point on three sides, where there are tidepools and a beautiful coastline.

Driving directions: From Highway 101 in Goleta, exit onto Ward Memorial Boulevard/Highway 217. Continue 2 miles to the Sandspit Road exit, and turn left at the stop sign, heading towards Goleta Beach Park. Drive 0.3 miles to the beach parking lot turnoff. Turn right and cross the lagoon into the parking lot.

Hiking directions: Hike west along the park lawn to the bluffs overlooking the ocean. Continue past the natural bridge. The path parallels the cliff edge into the university. At the marine laboratory, take the right fork, crossing the road to the UCSB Lagoon. The lagoon sits on Goleta Point. Take the path to the right around the northeast side of the lagoon. At the north end, the trail joins a walking path in the university. At the west end of the lagoon, the trail heads south on the return portion of the loop. Once back at the ocean, climb up the bluff to the left. Continue around the lagoon, and descend the steps between the lagoon and the ocean. Complete the loop back at the marine laboratory and bluffs. Head east, back to Goleta Beach County Park.

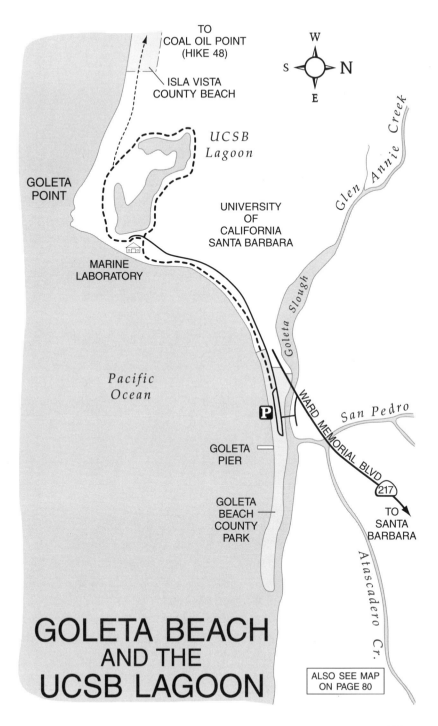

TO
COAL OIL POINT
(HIKE 48)

ISLA VISTA
COUNTY BEACH

W

S ✦ N

E

UCSB
Lagoon

Glen Annie Creek

GOLETA
POINT

UNIVERSITY
OF
CALIFORNIA
SANTA BARBARA

MARINE
LABORATORY

Goleta Slough

Pacific
Ocean

P

San Pedro

WARD MEMORIAL BLVD

GOLETA
PIER

217

TO
SANTA
BARBARA

GOLETA
BEACH
COUNTY
PARK

Atascadero Cr.

GOLETA BEACH
AND THE
UCSB LAGOON

ALSO SEE MAP
ON PAGE 80

Hike 48
Coal Oil Point Reserve

Hiking distance: 3 miles round trip
Hiking time: 1.5 hours
Elevation gain: Near level
Maps: U.S.G.S. Goleta and Dos Pueblos Canyon
        The Thomas Guide—Santa Barbara and Vicinity

Summary of hike: Coal Oil Point Reserve has several coastal wildlife habitats set aside for research, education and preservation. The 117-acre ecological study enclave, managed by UCSB, has coastal dunes, eucalyptus groves, grasslands, a salt marsh and a 45-acre lagoon. The trail parallels the bluffs from the western edge of Isla Vista to the reserve. Devereaux Lagoon, with a mixture of fresh water and salt water, provides several coastal lagoon habitats. The slough is a bird-watcher's paradise with a wide variety of native and migratory species.

Driving directions: From Santa Barbara, drive northbound on Highway 101 to the Glen Annie Road/Storke Road exit in Goleta. Turn left on Storke Road, and drive 1.3 miles to El Colegio Road. Turn left and drive 0.2 miles to Camino Corto. Turn right and continue 0.5 miles to Del Playa Drive. Turn right and park in the parking area at the end of the block.

Hiking directions: Take the well-defined path to the ocean bluffs and a T-junction. To the left, a stairway descends to the beach, and the blufftop path continues 0.2 miles east to Del Playa Park and Isla Vista County Beach. Take the right fork, parallel to the edge of the cliffs, and pass through a eucalyptus grove. Several surfing paths lead down the cliffs to the sandy beach and tidepools. The main trail leads to the Coal Oil Point Reserve. Pass through the habitat gate to Sands Beach. Several paths meander across the dunes to Devereaux Lagoon. A path circles the lagoon, returning on the paved roadway along the east side of the slough. You may also follow the beach for another mile northwest to the Ellwood Bluffs (Hikes 50 and 51).

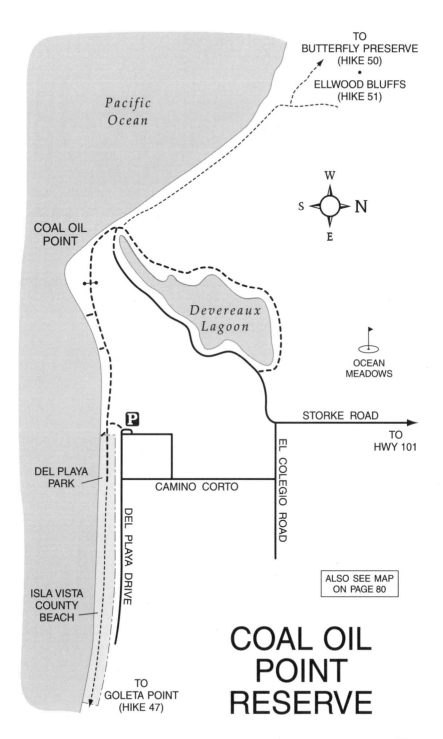

TO
BUTTERFLY PRESERVE
(HIKE 50)

• ELLWOOD BLUFFS
(HIKE 51)

*Pacific
Ocean*

COAL OIL
POINT

*Devereaux
Lagoon*

OCEAN
MEADOWS

STORKE ROAD

TO
HWY 101

EL COLEGIO ROAD

P

DEL PLAYA
PARK

CAMINO CORTO

DEL PLAYA DRIVE

ALSO SEE MAP
ON PAGE 80

ISLA VISTA
COUNTY
BEACH

TO
GOLETA POINT
(HIKE 47)

COAL OIL
POINT
RESERVE

Hike 49
Los Carneros County Park

Hiking distance: 1.5-mile loop
Hiking time: 1 hour
Elevation gain: Level
Maps: U.S.G.S. Goleta
       The Thomas Guide—Santa Barbara & Vicinity

Summary of hike: Los Carneros County Park is a nature preserve and bird habitat with a large 25-acre lake. A network of trails meander across the park through rolling meadows and a forest of eucalyptus, oak and pine trees. A wooden bridge crosses the northern end of the lake. At the trailhead is the Stow House, a Victorian home built in 1872, and the South Coast Railroad Museum, the original Goleta Train Station built in 1901. Both offer tours and exhibits.

Driving directions: From Santa Barbara, drive northbound on Highway 101 to Los Carneros Road in Goleta. Turn right and drive 0.3 miles north to the Stow House and Railroad Museum parking lot on the right. Turn right and park.

Hiking directions: From the parking lot, follow the rail fence past the Stow House. Continue straight ahead, following the sign to Los Carneros Lake and a junction. Take the paved path to the right. The path overlooks the lake. At the south end of the lake, a trail leads to the left and down to the lakeshore. Follow the shoreline around the southern end of the lake before heading up along the lake's east side. As you head north, the Santa Ynez Mountains are in full view. A variety of trails loop around the park, intersecting with each other. As you approach the north end of the lake, cross a wooden bridge over the willow and reed wetland. After crossing, the trail leads to the paved road near the trailhead. Head to the right, back to the parking lot.

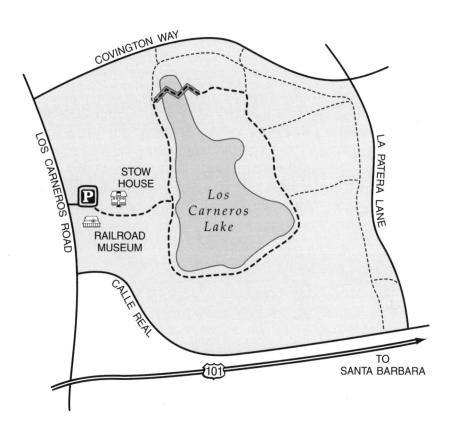

LOS CARNEROS
COUNTY PARK

Hike 50
Coronado Butterfly Preserve and
Ellwood Main Monarch Grove

Hiking distance: 1 mile round trip
Hiking time: 30 minutes
Elevation gain: 40 feet
Maps: U.S.G.S. Dos Pueblos Canyon

Summary of hike: The Coronado Butterfly Preserve was established as a nature preserve by the Land Trust for Santa Barbara in 1998. The 9.3-acre preserve and the Ellwood Main Monarch Grove are among the largest monarch butterfly wintering sites in southern California. Thousands of monarch butterflies hang from the eucalyptus trees in thick clusters and fly wildly around. The peak season for the migrating butterfly runs from December through February. Within the small preserve are woodlands, meadows and a creek. Trails connect the two preserves with the Ellwood Bluffs and beach to the west (Hike 51) and Devereaux Lagoon and Coal Oil Point Reserve to the east (Hike 48).

Driving directions: From Santa Barbara, drive northbound on Highway 101 to the Glen Annie Road/Storke Road exit in Goleta. Turn left on Storke Road, and drive 0.3 miles to Hollister Avenue, the first intersection. Turn right and continue 1.1 mile to Coronado Drive. Turn left and go 0.3 miles to the posted butterfly preserve on the right. Park alongside the street.

Hiking directions: Follow the wide path up the hill to the monarch butterfly information station. Gently descend into the large eucalyptus grove in the heart of the Coronado Butterfly Preserve. Cross a footbridge over seasonal Devereaux Creek to a T-junction. The right fork meanders through the grove to the west, connecting with the Ellwood Bluffs trails (Hike 51). Bear left and head deeper into the grove to another junction. The left fork returns to the south end of Coronado Drive. Take the right fork, meandering through the Ellwood Main Monarch

Grove. Climb up the hill through the towering eucalypti to an expansive open meadow. A network of interconnecting trails weaves across the bluffs. At the south edge of the 80-foot ocean bluffs, the left fork leads to Devereaux Lagoon and Coal Oil Point Reserve. The right fork heads west, connecting with Ellwood Bluffs.

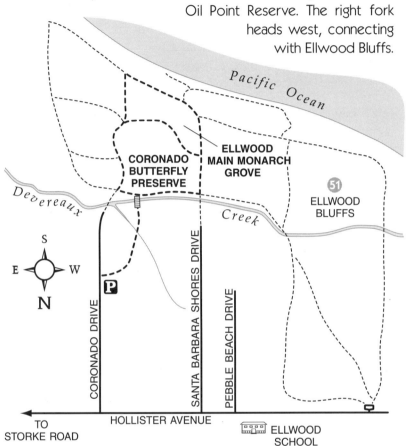

ALSO SEE MAP
ON PAGE 80

CORONADO
BUTTERFLY PRESERVE
ELLWOOD MAIN MONARCH
GROVE

Hike 51
Ellwood Bluffs Trail
SANTA BARBARA SHORES COUNTY PARK

Hiking distance: 3.5 miles round trip
Hiking time: 1.5 hours
Elevation gain: Level
Maps: U.S.G.S. Dos Pueblos Canyon
Santa Barbara County Recreational Map Series #8

Summary of hike: Santa Barbara Shores County Park has a network of interconnecting trails across flat grasslands overlooking the Pacific Ocean. The Ellwood Bluffs Trail parallels 80-foot high cliffs along the ocean's edge. The eucalyptus groves here are home to monarch butterflies during the winter months.

Driving directions: From Santa Barbara, drive northbound on Highway 101 to the Glen Annie Road/Storke Road exit in Goleta. Turn left on Storke Road, and drive 0.3 miles to Hollister Avenue, the first intersection. Turn right and continue 1.7 miles to the Santa Barbara County Park parking lot on the left, just past Ellwood School.

Hiking directions: At the trailhead is a junction. Take the right fork along the western edge of the parkland. The trail parallels a row of mature eucalyptus trees separating the Santa Barbara Shores County Park from the Sandpiper Golf Course. Continue south to the bluffs overlooking the ocean. Follow the trail to the left along the cliff's edge. Several trails cut across the open space to the left, returning to the trailhead for a shorter hike. At 0.5 miles is a junction with a beach access trail heading down to the mile-long beach. Further along the bluffs, take the trail inland, heading north along a row of eucalyptus trees. As you approach the eucalyptus groves, return along the prominent footpath to the left. The trail returns to the trailhead on the edge of the open meadows next to the groves.

To extend the hike, stroll through the eucalyptus groves along Devereaux Creek, connecting to the Ellwood Main

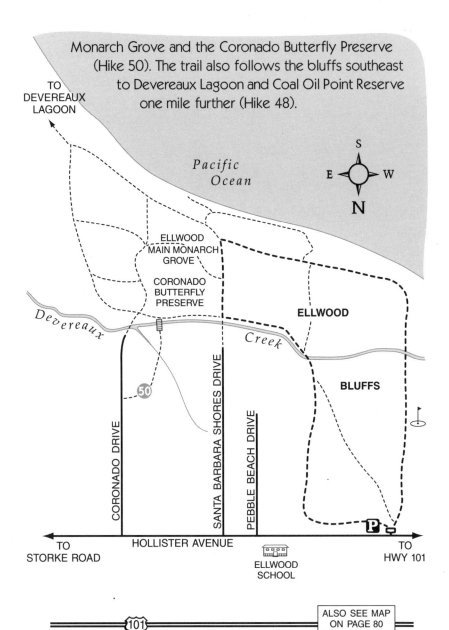

Monarch Grove and the Coronado Butterfly Preserve (Hike 50). The trail also follows the bluffs southeast to Devereaux Lagoon and Coal Oil Point Reserve one mile further (Hike 48).

TO DEVEREAUX LAGOON

Pacific Ocean

ELLWOOD MAIN MONARCH GROVE

CORONADO BUTTERFLY PRESERVE

Devereaux

ELLWOOD

Creek

BLUFFS

50

CORONADO DRIVE

SANTA BARBARA SHORES DRIVE

PEBBLE BEACH DRIVE

TO STORKE ROAD

HOLLISTER AVENUE

ELLWOOD SCHOOL

TO HWY 101

ALSO SEE MAP ON PAGE 80

101

ELLWOOD BLUFFS
SANTA BARBARA SHORES
COUNTY PARK

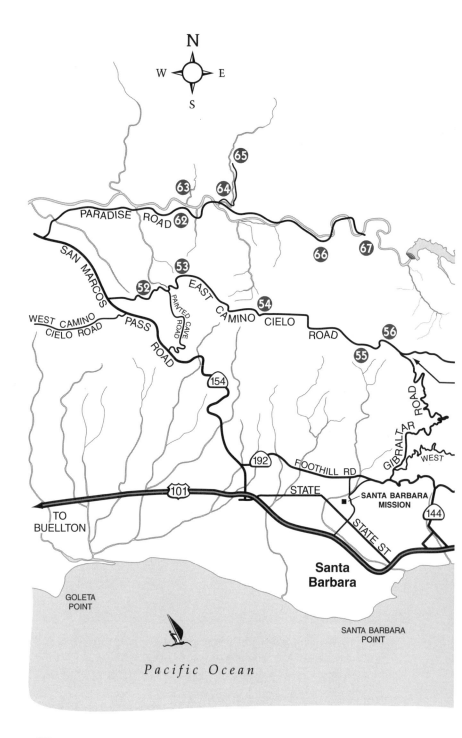

N
W E
S

65
63 64
PARADISE ROAD 62
66 67
SAN MARCOS
53
52 EAST CAMINO CIELO
54
PAINTED CAVE ROAD
WEST CAMINO CIELO ROAD
PASS ROAD
ROAD
56
55
GIBRALTAR ROAD
154
WEST
192 FOOTHILL RD
101 STATE
SANTA BARBARA MISSION
TO BUELLTON
STATE ST
144
Santa Barbara
GOLETA POINT
SANTA BARBARA POINT
Pacific Ocean

THE UPPER COUNTRY
HIKES 52–67
East Camino Cielo Road
Santa Ynez River Valley

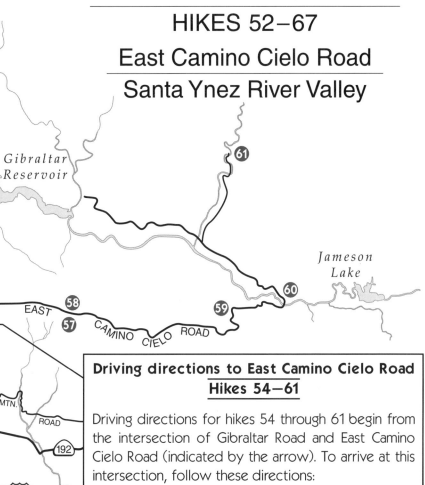

Gibraltar Reservoir

Jameson Lake

61

60

58

59

57

EAST

C*AMINO* C*IELO* ROAD

MTN.

ROAD

192

101

TO VENTURA

Driving directions to East Camino Cielo Road
Hikes 54–61

Driving directions for hikes 54 through 61 begin from the intersection of Gibraltar Road and East Camino Cielo Road (indicated by the arrow). To arrive at this intersection, follow these directions:

From the Santa Barbara Mission, take Mission Canyon Road north towards the mountains for 0.6 miles to Foothill Road—turn right. Drive 0.8 miles to West Mountain Drive and turn left. Continue 0.4 miles, bearing left at a road split while staying on West Mountain Drive. Continue 0.2 miles to Gibraltar Road and bear to the right. Begin winding and climbing for 6.5 miles up the mountain road to East Camino Cielo Road.

Hike 52
Fremont Ridge Trail

Hiking distance: 4 miles round trip
Hiking time: 2 hours
Elevation gain: 800 feet
Maps: U.S.G.S. San Marcos Pass
Santa Barbara Front Country Recreational Map

Summary of hike: The Fremont Trail is a vehicle-restricted road that winds down a ridge that divides two canyons. The trail overlooks the Santa Ynez River Valley, passing sandstone formations and a series of knolls. There are great views from the mountainous interior, including Lake Cachuma and Figueroa Mountain to the west, the national forest to the north, and the Pacific Ocean and Channel Islands to the south.

Driving directions: From Highway 101 in Santa Barbara, take the State Street/Highway 154 exit. Turn right on Highway 154 (San Marcos Pass Road), and drive 7.8 miles to East Camino Cielo Road on the right. Turn right and continue 1.6 miles to a Forest Service gate on the left. Parking pullouts are on the left past the trailhead gate.

Hiking directions: Hike past the Forest Service gate and head downhill. The trail follows the ridge that overlooks Los Laureles Canyon and Lake Cachuma to the west, the Santa Ynez River Valley below, and the Los Padres National Forest beyond. After the initial half-mile descent, the trail levels out. At one mile the trail begins a second descent and curves to the west. The trail passes under utility poles at two miles. This is a good turnaround point before the trail drops steeply to the Santa Ynez River Valley at Paradise Road. Return along the same trail.

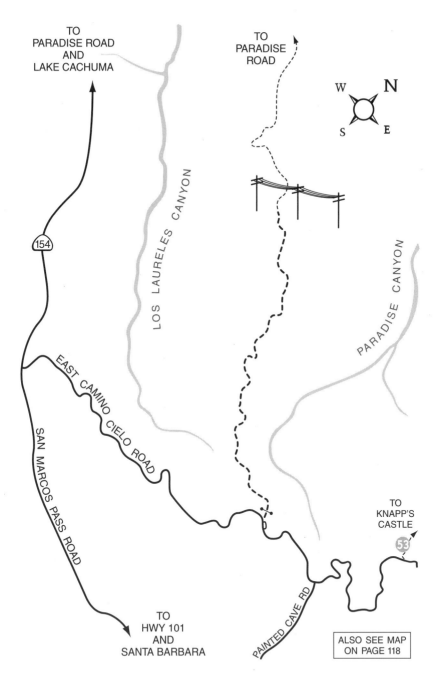

TO
PARADISE ROAD
AND
LAKE CACHUMA

TO
PARADISE
ROAD

W N S E

154

LOS LAURELES CANYON

PARADISE CANYON

EAST CAMINO CIELO ROAD

SAN MARCOS PASS ROAD

TO
KNAPP'S
CASTLE

53

TO
HWY 101
AND
SANTA BARBARA

PAINTED CAVE RD

ALSO SEE MAP
ON PAGE 118

FREMONT RIDGE TRAIL

Hike 53
Knapp's Castle
from East Camino Cielo Road

Hiking distance: 0.8 miles round trip
Hiking time: 30 minutes
Elevation gain: 100 feet
Maps: U.S.G.S. San Marcos Pass
      Santa Barbara Front Country Recreational Map

Summary of hike: Knapp's Castle is a stone ruin that sits on a rocky point with stunning vistas. An easy half-mile hike from East Camino Cielo Road leads to the 1916 sandstone mansion. The remains include the foundation, rock arches, fireplaces, chimneys and rock stairways. The rest of the castle was consumed in the 1940 Paradise Canyon Fire. The spectacular views extend up and down the Santa Ynez River Valley from Gibraltar Reservoir to Lake Cachuma. Although the castle sits on private property, the current owner graciously allows access. Knapp's Castle may also be reached from the Snyder Trail—Hike 62.

Driving directions: From Highway 101 in Santa Barbara, take the State Street/Highway 154 exit. Turn right on Highway 154 (San Marcos Pass Road), and drive 7.8 miles to East Camino Cielo Road on the right. Turn right and continue 3 miles to a Forest Service gate on the left, 0.9 miles past Painted Cave Road. Parking pullouts are on the right side of the road.

Hiking directions: Cross East Camino Cielo Road and hike north past the Forest Service "private property" gate. The trail, an unpaved road, crosses the hillside through chaparral to a trail split at 0.4 miles. The left fork is the Snyder Trail, leading three miles down to Paradise Road in the Santa Ynez River Valley (Hike 62). Bear to the right past a second "private property" gate. In less than a half mile, the castle ruins come into view on a point overlooking the river valley and the San Rafael Mountains. After walking through the ruins and marveling at the views, return along the same path.

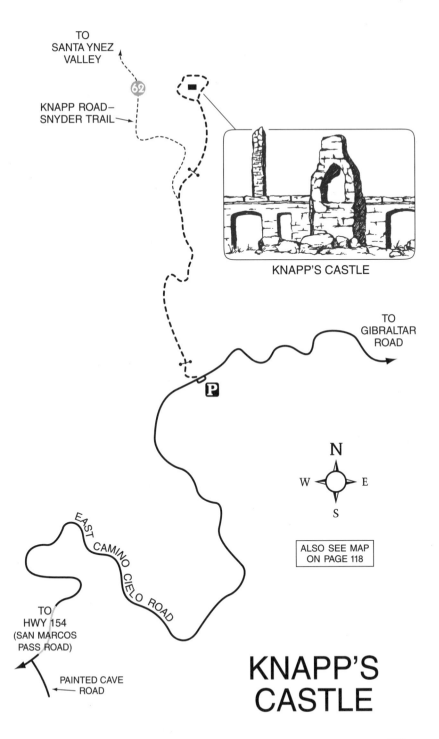

TO
SANTA YNEZ
VALLEY

62

KNAPP ROAD–
SNYDER TRAIL

KNAPP'S CASTLE

TO
GIBRALTAR
ROAD

P

N
W   E
S

ALSO SEE MAP
ON PAGE 118

EAST CAMINO CIELO ROAD

TO
HWY 154
(SAN MARCOS
PASS ROAD)

PAINTED CAVE
ROAD

KNAPP'S
CASTLE

Hike 54
Arroyo Burro Loop

Hiking distance: 6.5 mile loop
Hiking time: 3.5 hours
Elevation gain: 1,700 feet
Maps: U.S.G.S. San Marcos Pass and Little Pine Mountain
Santa Barbara Front Country Recreational Map

Summary of hike: The Arroyo Burro Trail, originally a Chumash Indian route, leads down a narrow, rocky canyon with a year-round stream. The trail connects with the Arroyo Burro Road just south of White Oak Camp. The loop hike returns along the winding Arroyo Burro Road, an unpaved, vehicle-restricted road.

Driving directions: From the intersection of Gibraltar Road and East Camino Cielo Road (see page 119), drive 4.9 miles west on East Camino Cielo Road to an unpaved road on the right. Turn right and head north 0.1 mile to a locked gate and parking pullouts.

From Highway 154 (San Marcos Pass Road), drive 6.2 miles east on East Camino Cielo Road to the turnoff on the left.

Hiking directions: Hike north past the locked gate on the graded Arroyo Burro Road. A hundred yards past the gate is a signed junction for the Arroyo Burro Trail on the left. Leave the road and head downhill to the left on the footpath. This is the beginning of the loop, as you will return on the graded road. The trail quickly descends into the narrow Arroyo Burro Canyon and crosses the stream several times. At three miles, the trail rejoins the Arroyo Burro Road just above White Oak Camp, less than a mile from the Santa Ynez River. For the return, take the winding dirt road along the east canyon wall 3.5 miles back to the trailhead.

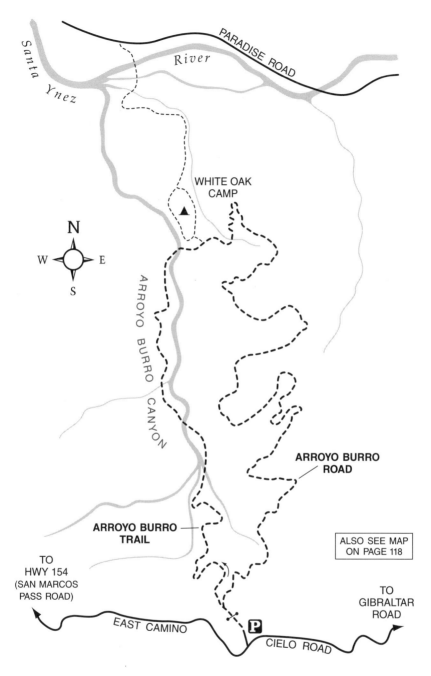

PARADISE ROAD

Santa Ynez

River

WHITE OAK
CAMP

N
W E
S

ARROYO BURRO CANYON

ARROYO BURRO
ROAD

ARROYO BURRO
TRAIL

ALSO SEE MAP
ON PAGE 118

TO
HWY 154
(SAN MARCOS
PASS ROAD)

TO
GIBRALTAR
ROAD

P

EAST CAMINO

CIELO ROAD

ARROYO BURRO LOOP

Hike 55
La Cumbre Vista Point

Hiking distance: 0.3 to 0.8 miles round trip
Hiking time: 30 minutes
Elevation gain: 100 feet
Maps: U.S.G.S. Santa Barbara

Summary of hike: Although this is a short hike, it is a magical location and well worth the stop. The loop trail leads to La Cumbre Peak, the highest peak in the Santa Ynez Mountains. From the 3,985-foot summit are panoramic coastal vistas from Point Magu in the Santa Monica Mountains to Point Conception. Cathedral Peak can be seen a short half mile to the south and 650 feet lower. The unobstructed views of Santa Barbara and the coastline are superb. A paved path loops around the old fire lookout tower. The abandoned tower is fenced off and currently a satellite station.

Driving directions: From the intersection of Gibraltar Road and East Camino Cielo Road (see page 119), drive 1.9 miles west on East Camino Cielo Road to the signed trailhead and parking pullouts on the left side.
From Highway 154 (San Marcos Pass Road), drive 9.2 miles east on East Camino Cielo Road to the trailhead and parking pullouts on the right.

Hiking directions: From the parking pullout, hike up the gated, asphalt road past the pine trees to a junction. Take the right fork and return on the left fork. At the first overlook is a bench. Footpaths lead down to large, sculpted sandstone boulders and additional overlooks. Continue on the winding road, heading east to a second overlook with benches. Again, footpaths lead downhill to more overlooks. The main trail loops around, passing the fenced satellite station, back to the trailhead.

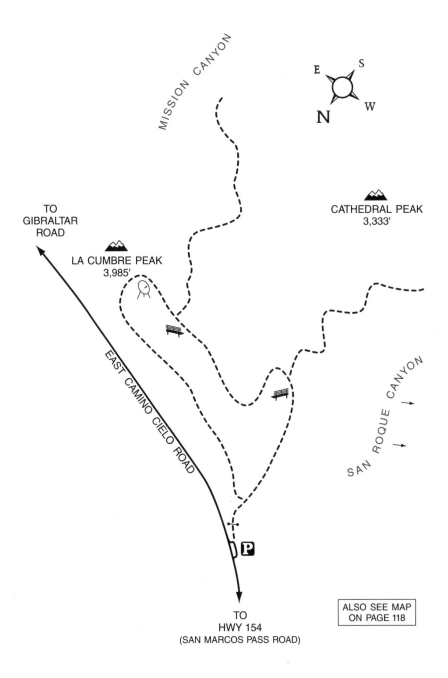

MISSION CANYON

E · S
N · W

TO
GIBRALTAR
ROAD

CATHEDRAL PEAK
3,333'

LA CUMBRE PEAK
3,985'

EAST CAMINO CIELO ROAD

SAN ROQUE CANYON

P

TO
HWY 154
(SAN MARCOS PASS ROAD)

ALSO SEE MAP
ON PAGE 118

LA CUMBRE VISTA POINT

Hike 56
Angostura Pass Road

Hiking distance: 3 to 14 miles round trip
Hiking time: 1.5 to 7 hours
Elevation gain: 1,000 to 2,000 feet
Maps: U.S.G.S. Santa Barbara and Little Pine Mountain
Santa Barbara Front Country Recreational Map

Summary of hike: The Angostura Pass Road is a service road that leads seven miles down the north face of the Santa Ynez Mountains to Gibraltar Dam. The hike down the road overlooks Gibraltar Reservoir and the dam. There are great views across the Santa Ynez River Valley of Little Pine and Big Pine Mountains. Along the way, the Matias Potrero Trail connects the Angostura Pass Road with the Arroyo Burro Road (Hike 54). You may walk as long as you prefer, returning back along the same road.

Driving directions: From the intersection of Gibraltar Road and East Camino Cielo Road (see page 119), drive 0.7 miles west on East Camino Cielo Road to an unpaved road and parking pull-out on the right.

From Highway 154 (San Marcos Pass Road), drive 10.4 miles east on East Camino Cielo Road to the parking pullout on the left.

Hiking directions: Take the graded road 100 yards north to the locked gate. Continue past the gate for about a mile to a signed junction with the steep Matias Potrero Trail, a footpath heading down to the left. Stay on the road as it heads east across the contours of the mountain. At two miles, the trail begins heading around Devils Canyon. As you look across the mountainside, the road can be seen winding its way down to Gibraltar Dam. Choose your own turnaround spot anywhere along the road.

To begin the hike from Gibraltar Dam, drive to the end of Paradise Road, following the driving directions for High 67. Take the High Road for 2.6 miles to Angostura Pass Road.

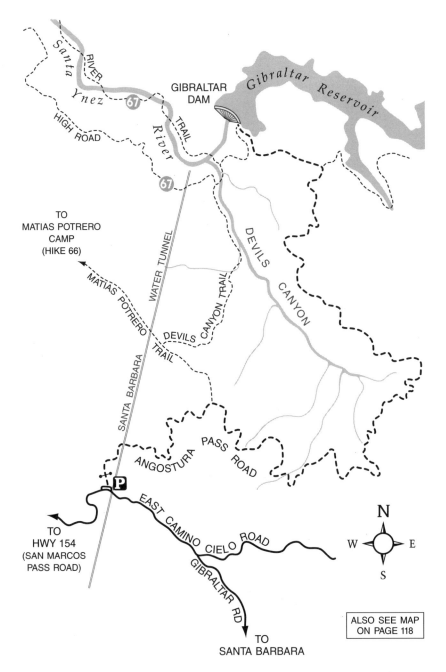

Santa Ynez River

RIVER

67

HIGH ROAD

GIBRALTAR DAM

Gibraltar Reservoir

TRAIL

River

67

TO
MATIAS POTRERO
CAMP
(HIKE 66)

WATER TUNNEL

MATIAS POTRERO TRAIL

DEVILS CANYON TRAIL

SANTA BARBARA TRAIL

DEVILS CANYON

ANGOSTURA PASS ROAD

P

EAST CAMINO CIELO ROAD

TO
HWY 154
(SAN MARCOS
PASS ROAD)

GIBRALTAR RD

N
W   E
S

ALSO SEE MAP
ON PAGE 118

TO
SANTA BARBARA

ANGOSTURA PASS ROAD

Hike 57
Montecito Peak
Cold Spring Trail

Hiking distance: 4 miles round trip
Hiking time: 2 hours
Elevation gain: 700 feet
Maps: U.S.G.S. Santa Barbara
Santa Barbara Front Country Recreational Map

Summary of hike: This hike leads to Montecito Peak, a bald, dome-shaped mountain with a 3,214-foot summit and a diameter of about 50 feet. There are magnificent 360-degree views of the coastal communities and the ocean. The hike begins at the top of the Santa Ynez Mountains on East Camino Cielo Road and descends 700 feet down the south face of the mountains. Montecito Peak can also be reached from the East Fork of Cold Spring Canyon (Hike 32).

Driving directions: From the intersection of Gibraltar Road and East Camino Cielo Road (see page 119), drive 3.6 miles east on East Camino Cielo Road. The trailhead parking area is on the right side of the road by a large cement water tank.

Hiking directions: From the parking area, take the Cold Spring Trail heading south on the right side of the water tank. The well-defined path overlooks Santa Barbara, the ocean and the Channel Islands as it heads downhill. At the head of Cold Spring Canyon, the trail curves around the mountainside towards the prominent Montecito Peak. At 1.2 miles, the trail approaches the northwest side of the dome, then skirts around the western edge of the mountain, heading down to the East Fork of Cold Spring Canyon. As you near the dome, watch for a steep and narrow unmarked path on the left. Take this path to a ridge. From here, it is a short, but steep, 200-foot scramble to the summit. Careful footing is a must! Return on the same trail to the road and parking lot.

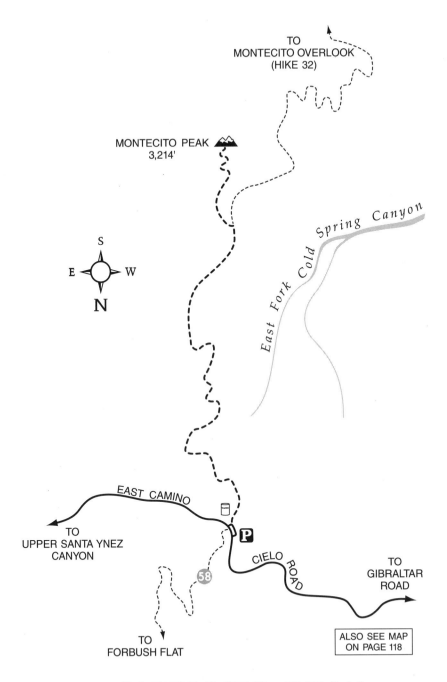

TO
MONTECITO OVERLOOK
(HIKE 32)

MONTECITO PEAK
3,214'

East Fork Cold Spring Canyon

S

E — W

N

EAST CAMINO

TO
UPPER SANTA YNEZ
CANYON

P

58

CIELO ROAD

TO
GIBRALTAR
ROAD

TO
FORBUSH FLAT

ALSO SEE MAP
ON PAGE 118

MONTECITO PEAK

Hike 58
Forbush Flat
Cold Spring Trail

Hiking distance: 4 miles round trip
Hiking time: 2.5 hours
Elevation gain: 1,000 feet
Maps: U.S.G.S. Santa Barbara
       Santa Barbara Front Country Recreational Map

Summary of hike: This hike descends a thousand feet down the north slope of the Santa Ynez Mountains to Forbush Flat, a beautiful meadow located by Gidney Creek. Forbush Flat was the location of Fred Forbush's old homestead from the early 1900s. The only remnant of the homestead is an aging fruit tree orchard. From the flat, the trail continues west down Forbush Canyon and north to the Santa Ynez River.

Driving directions: From the intersection of Gibraltar Road and East Camino Cielo Road (see page 119), drive 3.6 miles east on East Camino Cielo Road. The trailhead parking area is on the right side of the road by a large cement water tank.

Hiking directions: Cross East Camino Cielo Road to the Cold Spring Trail. Head steeply downhill on the west side of the canyon. At 0.5 miles, after a few switchbacks, the trail crosses a seasonal stream to a bench. Continue downhill along the chaparral covered canyon wall. At one mile, the trail opens up to beautiful vistas of the Santa Ynez Valley and the mountains beyond. From here, look back up the canyon. When the creek is flowing, a 25-foot waterfall cascades off the rock wall. At two miles, the trail reaches Forbush Flat. The orchard, meadow and campsites are on the left. The main trail continues a short distance down a series of switchbacks to Gidney Creek and a junction. The right fork leads two miles to Cottam Camp and Blue Canyon (Hike 59). Straight ahead, the trail leads another two miles to the Santa Ynez River. To return, take the same trail back.

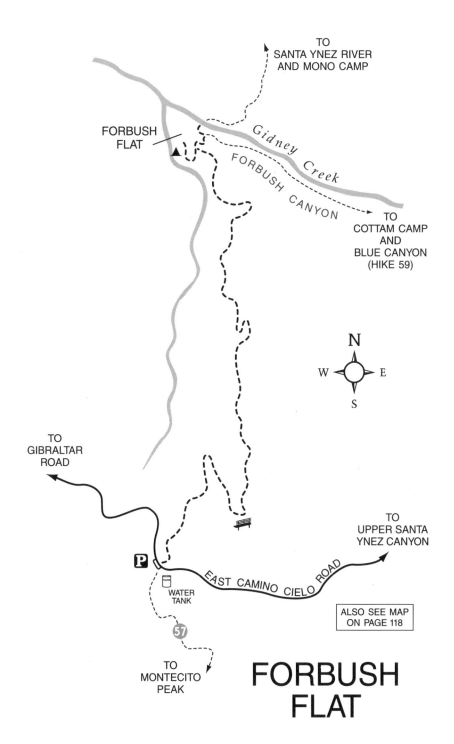

TO
SANTA YNEZ RIVER
AND MONO CAMP

FORBUSH
FLAT

Gidney Creek

FORBUSH CANYON

TO
COTTAM CAMP
AND
BLUE CANYON
(HIKE 59)

N
W E
S

TO
GIBRALTAR
ROAD

TO
UPPER SANTA
YNEZ CANYON

EAST CAMINO CIELO ROAD

P

WATER
TANK

ALSO SEE MAP
ON PAGE 118

57

TO
MONTECITO
PEAK

FORBUSH
FLAT

Hike 59
Blue Canyon

Hiking distance: 3.2 miles round trip
Hiking time: 1.5 hours
Elevation gain: 200 feet
Maps: U.S.G.S. Carpinteria
Santa Barbara Front Country Recreational Map

Summary of hike: The Blue Canyon Trail follows Escondido Creek through a narrow canyon past weathered sandstone outcroppings and blue-green serpentine rock. The small, lush canyon has stands of oak, sycamore and alder trees. The trail leads to Upper Blue Canyon Camp, a primitive camp along the banks of a stream near pools and cascades.

Driving directions: From the intersection of Gibraltar Road and East Camino Cielo Road (see page 119), drive 10.4 east miles on East Camino Cielo Road to the trailhead and parking pullout on the left.

Hiking directions: Hike west along the north canyon wall, immediately dropping into Blue Canyon. At 0.3 miles and again at 0.6 miles, the trail passes a series of beautifully eroded sandstone formations. The trail gradually descends to Escondido Creek and the forested canyon floor at one mile. Cross the creek and continue downstream to a small stream crossing at 1.5 miles. Cross the stream to Upper Blue Canyon Camp on a small flat above the water. A short distance beyond the camp is another crossing of Escondido Creek. This is the turnaround spot.

To hike further, the trail continues through the canyon another 3.5 miles to a large oak-dotted meadow at Cottam Camp and 5.5 miles to Forbush Flat (Hike 58).

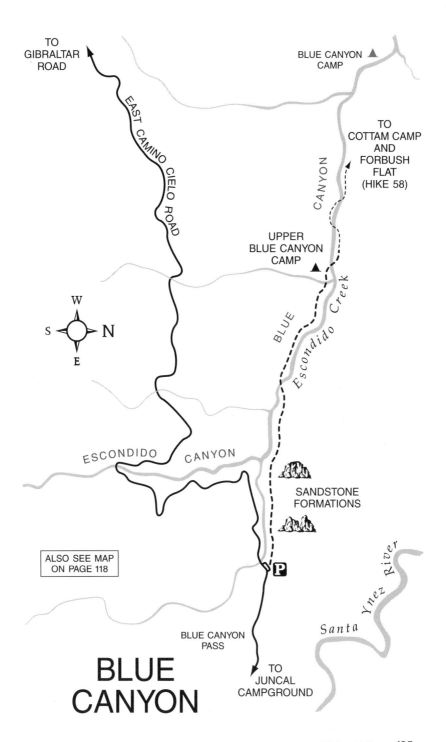

TO
GIBRALTAR
ROAD

BLUE CANYON
CAMP

EAST CAMINO CIELO ROAD

TO
COTTAM CAMP
AND
FORBUSH
FLAT
(HIKE 58)

CANYON

UPPER
BLUE CANYON
CAMP

W
S N
E

BLUE

Escondido Creek

ESCONDIDO   CANYON

SANDSTONE
FORMATIONS

ALSO SEE MAP
ON PAGE 118

P

Santa Ynez River

BLUE CANYON
PASS

BLUE
CANYON

TO
JUNCAL
CAMPGROUND

Hike 60
Jameson Lake

Hiking distance: 7 miles round trip
Hiking time: 3.5 hours
Elevation gain: 500 feet
Maps: U.S.G.S. Carpinteria and White Ledge Peak
Santa Barbara Front Country Recreational Map

Summary of hike: The hike to picturesque Jameson Lake heads up Juncal Canyon to the upper end of the Santa Ynez drainage. The trail follows the Santa Ynez River and parallels the south shore of the reservoir. There are great views down the Santa Ynez Valley to the west and to the upper canyon in the east.

Driving directions: From the intersection of Gibraltar Road and East Camino Cielo Road (see page 119), drive 12 miles east on East Camino Cielo Road to the Juncal Campground on the valley floor. Turn right, entering the campground, and continue straight ahead. Park at the far east end.

Hiking directions: At the far end of the Juncal Campground, head east past the gate on the unpaved Juncal Road. Cross the tributary stream and follow the near-level road through meadows dotted with oak trees. Head to the upper end of the canyon, parallel to the Santa Ynez River. The side trails lead down to the river. At 1.5 miles, cross the Santa Ynez River. After crossing, the trail begins a 300-foot ascent, curving up and around the west side of the mountain. Views open up to the east and west, including the first look at Jameson Lake. As you round the mountain towards the south, the trail continues above Alder Creek and parallel to the south shore of Jameson Lake. At 3.5 miles is a junction on the right with the Alder Creek trail. This is the turnaround spot.

To hike further, the trail leads down to Alder Creek and follows the creek past pools and small waterfalls to Alder Camp, one mile ahead. The main trail continues east along the lake to the Murrietta Divide and on to Matilija Creek at Ojai.

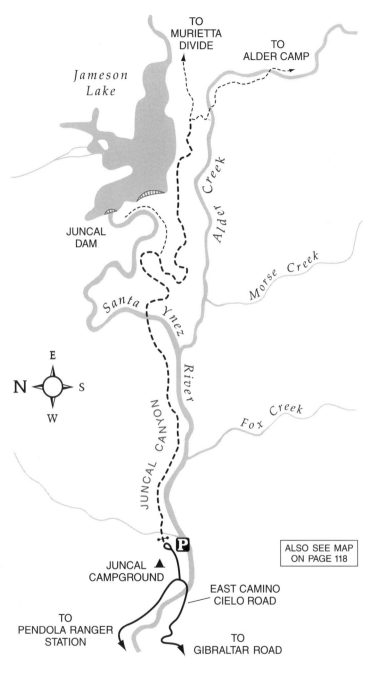

TO
MURIETTA
DIVIDE

TO
ALDER CAMP

*Jameson
Lake*

Alder Creek

Morse Creek

JUNCAL
DAM

Santa Ynez River

E
N ⊙ S
W

JUNCAL CANYON

Fox Creek

ALSO SEE MAP
ON PAGE 118

P

JUNCAL ▲
CAMPGROUND

EAST CAMINO
CIELO ROAD

TO
PENDOLA RANGER
STATION

TO
GIBRALTAR ROAD

JAMESON LAKE

Hike 61
Agua Caliente Canyon

Hiking distance: 4 miles round trip
Hiking time: 2 hours
Elevation gain: 200 feet
Maps: U.S.G.S. Hildreth Peak
       Santa Barbara Front Country map
       Dick Smith Wilderness map

Summary of hike: Agua Caliente, which means "hot water," is home to Big Caliente Hot Springs, a bathing pool near the trailhead that is perfect for soaking after the hike. The hike up Agua Caliente Canyon follows Agua Caliente Creek along an old pack trail, passing sandstone formations and Big Caliente Debris Dam. At the dam is an overlook of its 70-foot tall spillway.

Driving directions: From the intersection of Gibraltar Road and East Camino Cielo Road (see page 119), drive 12 miles east on East Camino Cielo Road to the Juncal Campground on the valley floor. Bear left and continue 3 miles to the Pendola Ranger Station at Big Caliente Road on the right. Turn right and drive 2.4 miles to Caliente Hot Springs. Park off the road.

Hiking directions: Follow the unpaved road up canyon past the cement hot springs pool. A short distance ahead, the road narrows to a footpath by a trail sign. The path parallels Agua Caliente Creek past a series of pools. At 0.5 miles, the trail crosses the creek and heads gently uphill to the Big Caliente Dam and the spillway overlook. Past the dam, the trail levels out through a lush, forested flat, staying close to the watercourse. The trail recrosses the creek at 1.6 miles near the mouth of Diablo Canyon on the right. Bear to the left, continuing deeper into Agua Caliente Canyon. At two miles the trail crosses the main creek and the canyon narrows. This is a good turnaround spot. To hike further, the Agua Caliente Trail continues for several miles up the canyon.

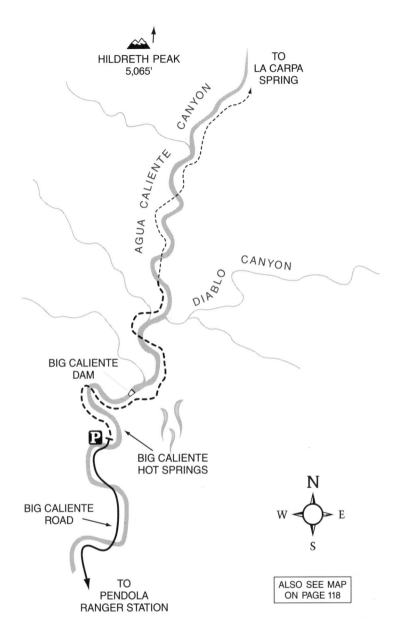

HILDRETH PEAK
5,065'

TO
LA CARPA
SPRING

AGUA CALIENTE CANYON

DIABLO CANYON

BIG CALIENTE
DAM

BIG CALIENTE
HOT SPRINGS

P

BIG CALIENTE
ROAD

N
W E
S

ALSO SEE MAP
ON PAGE 118

TO
PENDOLA
RANGER STATION

AGUA CALIENTE
CANYON

Hike 62
Knapp's Castle
from Snyder Trail

Hiking distance: 6.6 miles round trip
Hiking time: 3.5 hours
Elevation gain: 2,000 feet
Maps: U.S.G.S. San Marcos Pass
       Santa Barbara Front Country Recreational Map

Summary of hike: The Snyder Trail is a longer, steeper trail to Knapp's Castle than the easy stroll from East Camino Cielo Road (Hike 53). This route begins from Paradise Road in the Santa Ynez River Valley and heads up to the ridge alongside Lewis Canyon. The hike begins on a service road but narrows to a footpath. A brief description of Knapp's Castle is on page 120.

Driving directions: From Highway 101 in Santa Barbara, take the State Street/Highway 154 exit. Turn right on Highway 154 (San Marcos Pass Road), and drive 10.6 miles to Paradise Road on the right. Turn right and continue 4.2 miles to the turnout on the right by a "No Vehicle" gate. Park in the turnout. If you reach the Los Prietos Ranger Station, you have gone a little too far.

Hiking directions: From the turnout, hike past the gate on the unpaved road. Fifty yards ahead is the Snyder Trail sign. Stay on the service road past a water tank to a trail split at 0.3 miles. Bear to the right. At 0.7 miles is another water tank on the left and a trail split. Go left on the footpath. The trail gains elevation up several switchbacks through a forested area, then heads across grassy slopes and knolls. Along the way, the views get better and the knolls offer stopping spots. At 1.8 miles, the Snyder Trail joins Knapp Road at a junction. Take the road to the right as it curves around the contours of the hillside through a forest of oaks and bays. At 3.1 miles the trail joins an unpaved road that leads to East Camino Cielo Road. Take the unpaved road to the left, and pass the "private property" gate to Knapp's Castle. Return along the same route.

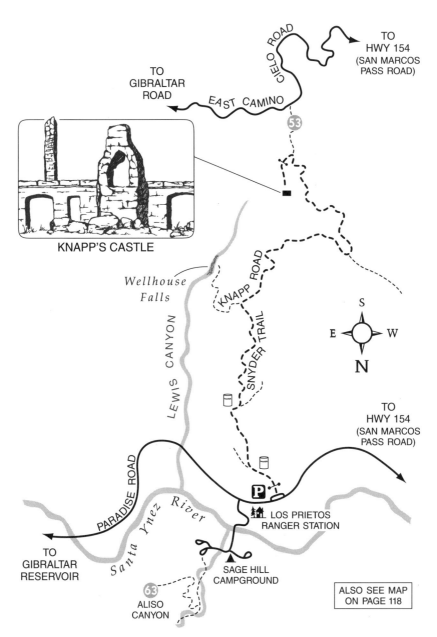

KNAPP'S CASTLE

TO
HWY 154
(SAN MARCOS
PASS ROAD)

CIELO ROAD

TO
GIBRALTAR
ROAD

EAST CAMINO

53

Wellhouse
Falls

KNAPP ROAD

SNYDER TRAIL

LEWIS CANYON

S
E — W
N

TO
HWY 154
(SAN MARCOS
PASS ROAD)

P

PARADISE ROAD

Santa Ynez River

LOS PRIETOS
RANGER STATION

TO
GIBRALTAR
RESERVOIR

SAGE HILL
CAMPGROUND

63

ALISO
CANYON

ALSO SEE MAP
ON PAGE 118

SNYDER TRAIL
TO KNAPP'S CASTLE

Hike 63
Aliso Canyon Loop Trail

Hiking distance: 3.5 mile loop
Hiking time: 2 hours
Elevation gain: 800 feet
Maps: U.S.G.S. San Marcos Pass
　　　　　Santa Barbara Front Country Recreational Map

Summary of hike: The Aliso Canyon Loop Trail begins on a one-mile interpretive trail along Aliso Creek, crossing and recrossing the creek continuously up stream. The trail climbs to a grassy plateau and continues across the hill that divides Aliso Canyon and Oso Canyon. The views overlook the Santa Ynez River Valley and the surrounding mountains.

Driving directions: From Highway 101 in Santa Barbara, take the State Street/Highway 154 exit. Turn right on Highway 154 (San Marcos Pass Road), and drive 10.6 miles to Paradise Road on the right. Turn right and continue 4.5 miles to the Los Prietos Ranger Station on the left. Turn left and follow the park road to the Sage Hill Campground. Park in the upper east end of the campground.

Hiking directions: Hike north into the forested canyon. At a quarter mile, after a few creek crossings, there is a junction with the Aliso Loop Trail, the return route. Continue straight ahead, crossing the creek numerous times and winding up the canyon. Just past sign post #15, the trail heads over a small sage covered hill before dropping back down to the creek. Cross the creek to a junction with the Aliso Loop Trail at one mile. Ascend the eastern hillside of the canyon to the right, away from the creek. The trail climbs steadily for a half mile to a grassy meadow and a junction with a trail heading left (east) to Upper Oso Campground (Hikes 64 and 65). Take the right fork, traversing the ridge that divides the canyons. Switchbacks descend back into Aliso Canyon. Rejoin the interpretive trail and return to the trailhead.

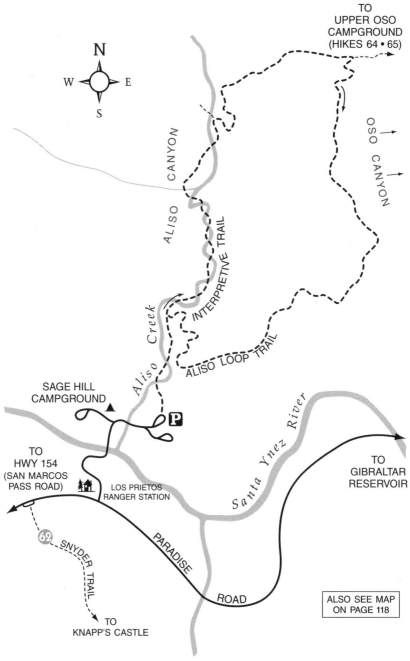

TO
UPPER OSO
CAMPGROUND
(HIKES 64 • 65)

N
W E
S

ALISO CANYON

OSO CANYON

INTERPRETIVE TRAIL

Aliso Creek

ALISO LOOP TRAIL

Santa Ynez River

SAGE HILL
CAMPGROUND

P

TO
HWY 154
(SAN MARCOS
PASS ROAD)

LOS PRIETOS
RANGER STATION

TO
GIBRALTAR
RESERVOIR

62 SNYDER TRAIL

PARADISE

ROAD

TO
KNAPP'S CASTLE

ALSO SEE MAP
ON PAGE 118

ALISO CANYON TRAIL

Hike 64
Lower Oso Trail

Hiking distance: 2 miles round trip
Hiking time: 1 hour
Elevation gain: 200 feet
Maps: U.S.G.S. San Marcos Pass
       Santa Barbara Front Country Recreational Map

Summary of hike: The Lower Oso Trail is a short meander at the mouth of Oso Canyon. The trail winds through a beautiful meadow along the banks of Oso Creek, connecting the Lower and Upper Oso Campgrounds.

Driving directions: From Highway 101 in Santa Barbara, take the State Street / Highway 154 exit. Turn right on Highway 154 (San Marcos Pass Road), and drive 10.6 miles to Paradise Road on the right. Turn right and continue 5.8 miles to the Lower Oso Campground on the left. The campground is just beyond the first crossing of the Santa Ynez River. Park in the lot on the right, across from the junction with Romero Camuesa Road.

Hiking directions: From the parking area, hike up the paved Romero Camuesa Road. Parallel Oso Creek towards Upper Oso Campground. At 0.3 miles, the road crosses a bridge over the creek. After crossing, leave the road on a footpath to the left. Cross Oso Creek and follow the path through the forested meadow along the west side of the creek. At 1.2 miles, the trail crosses the creek again and heads into the lower end of Upper Oso Campground. This is the turnaround spot.

    To extend the hike to Nineteen Oaks Camp at the base of Little Pine Mountain, continue with Hike 65, which begins in Upper Oso Campground.

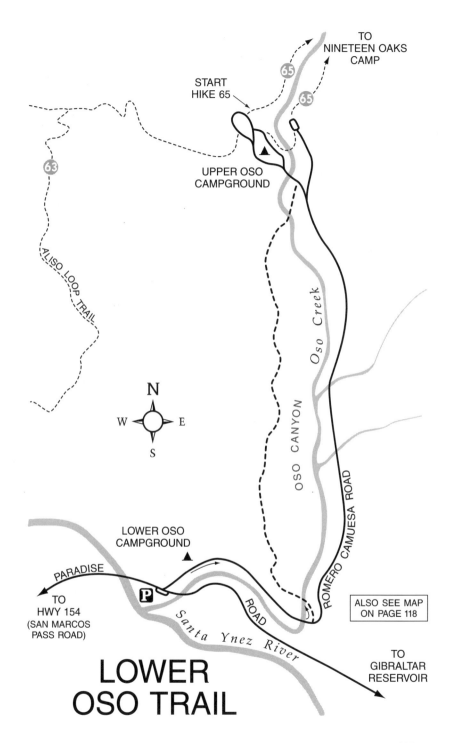

TO
NINETEEN OAKS
CAMP

65

65

START
HIKE 65

63

UPPER OSO
CAMPGROUND

ALISO LOOP TRAIL

Oso Creek

OSO CANYON

N

W E

S

ROMERO CAMUESA ROAD

LOWER OSO
CAMPGROUND

ALSO SEE MAP
ON PAGE 118

PARADISE

P

TO
HWY 154
(SAN MARCOS
PASS ROAD)

ROAD

Santa Ynez River

TO
GIBRALTAR
RESERVOIR

LOWER
OSO TRAIL

Hike 65
Oso Canyon to Nineteen Oaks Camp

Hiking distance: 4 miles round trip
Hiking time: 2 hours
Elevation gain: 700 feet
Maps: U.S.G.S. San Marcos Pass
       Santa Barbara Front Country Recreational Map

Summary of hike: The hike to Nineteen Oaks Camp follows Oso Canyon through the steep sandstone cliffs of Oso Narrows. The trail parallels Oso Creek up the canyon and past pools to the camp, located at the base of Little Pine Mountain. The camp sits on a shady knoll in an oak tree grove with picnic tables, fire pits and beautiful views down Oso Canyon.

Driving directions: Follow the driving directions for Hike 64. Turn left into Lower Oso Campground on Romero Camuesa Road, and drive one mile to the Upper Oso Campground. Head to the far end of the campground, past the horse corrals.

Hiking directions: Take the Canyon Trail past the gate, and enter the steep-walled canyon. At one mile, after several creek crossings, the lush trail intersects with the Santa Cruz Trail veering off to the left. Continue on the Santa Cruz Trail parallel to Oso Creek, crossing the creek a few more times past pools and cascades. Various side paths lead downhill to the pools. At 1.8 miles is a signed junction to Nineteen Oaks Camp. The main trail begins its ascent to the summit of Little Pine Mountain. Take the right fork a quarter mile uphill to Nineteen Oaks Camp, located on a knoll overlooking the canyon.

On the return route, stay on the Santa Cruz Trail until arriving at the Buckhorn Road junction, a short distance past the junction with the Canyon Trail. Take the unpaved Buckhorn Road to the right, returning to the lower end of the Upper Oso Campground. Return through the campground to the trailhead.

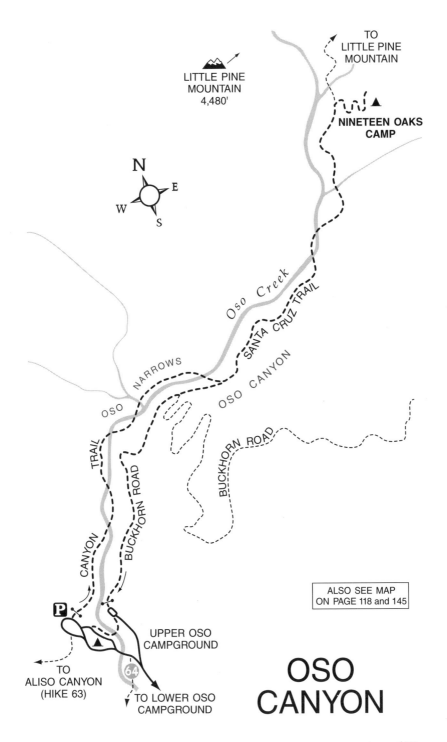

TO
LITTLE PINE
MOUNTAIN

LITTLE PINE
MOUNTAIN
4,480'

NINETEEN OAKS
CAMP

N
E
W
S

Oso Creek

SANTA CRUZ TRAIL

NARROWS

OSO CANYON

OSO

BUCKHORN ROAD

TRAIL

BUCKHORN ROAD

CANYON

ALSO SEE MAP
ON PAGE 118 and 145

P

UPPER OSO
CAMPGROUND

64

TO
ALISO CANYON
(HIKE 63)

TO LOWER OSO
CAMPGROUND

OSO
CANYON

Hike 66
Matias Potrero Trail

Hiking distance: 3 miles round trip
Hiking time: 1.5 hours
Elevation gain: 600 feet
Maps: U.S.G.S. Little Pine Mountain
      Santa Ynez Recreation Area map
      Santa Barbara Front Country Recreational Map

Summary of hike: The Matias Potrero Trail is a connector trail between Arroyo Burro Trail and Angostura Pass Road (Hikes 54 and 56). The picturesque trail follows the Santa Ynez Fault along the grassy north slopes of the Santa Ynez Mountains, passing meadows, rolling hills, canyons, rock formations and chaparral. The trail leads to Matias Potrero Camp, a primitive campsite in an oak grove with a picnic table and a rock cookstove.

Driving directions: From Highway 101 in Santa Barbara, take the State Street/Highway 154 exit. Turn right on Highway 154 (San Marcos Pass Road), and drive 10.6 miles to Paradise Road on the right. Turn right and continue 9 miles to the parking area on the left, across the road from the signed trailhead.

Hiking directions: Cross the road and head south past the trail sign and metal gate. Ascend a steep hill for the first 100 yards. Continue south along the ridge between two ravines. A stream flows through the drainage on the right. At 1.2 miles, the trail crosses under power poles to a signed junction. The right fork heads west to the Arroyo Burro Trail. Go east on the left fork, towards Gibraltar Road and Matias Potrero Camp, to a second junction at 0.2 miles. The right fork (the main trail) continues to Gibraltar Road. Take the left fork downhill to Matias Potrero Camp. The trail continues beyond the camp and rejoins the main trail. To return, take the same path back.

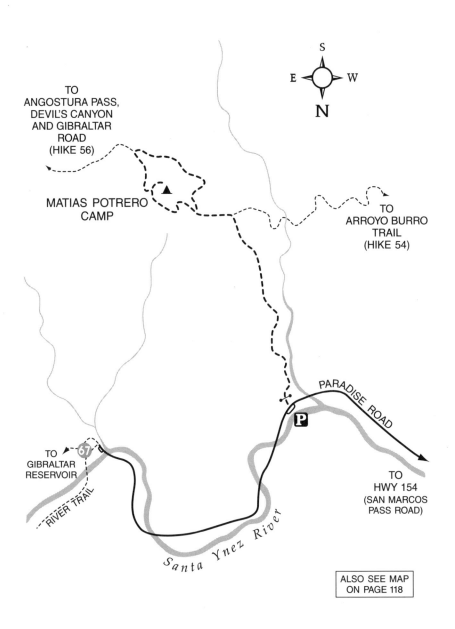

TO
ANGOSTURA PASS,
DEVIL'S CANYON
AND GIBRALTAR
ROAD
(HIKE 56)

MATIAS POTRERO
CAMP

S

E ⊕ W

N

TO
ARROYO BURRO
TRAIL
(HIKE 54)

PARADISE ROAD

P

TO
GIBRALTAR
RESERVOIR

TO
HWY 154
(SAN MARCOS
PASS ROAD)

RIVER TRAIL

Santa Ynez River

ALSO SEE MAP
ON PAGE 118

MATIAS POTRERO TRAIL

Hike 67
Red Rocks to Gibraltar Dam

Hiking distance: 6.5 miles round trip
Hiking time: 3 hours
Elevation gain: 500 feet
Maps: U.S.G.S. Little Pine Mountain
Santa Barbara Front Country Map

Summary of hike: The Red Rocks Trail follows the Santa Ynez River up the twisting canyon to Gibraltar Dam and the reservoir. Along the way there are numerous swimming holes and beautiful rock formations. Two routes lead to the dam, creating a loop hike. The Upper Road, known locally as the High Road, is a vehicle-restricted road that traverses the mountains overlooking the Santa Ynez River, the swimming holes and the surrounding hills. The River Trail, once a mining road, winds along the canyon floor with frequent river crossings. The River Trail can be difficult and is not recommended during high water. At that time, return along the High Road.

Driving directions: From Highway 101 in Santa Barbara, take the State Street/Highway 154 exit. Turn right on Highway 154 (San Marcos Pass Road), and drive 10.6 miles to Paradise Road on the right. Turn right and continue 10.4 miles to the trailhead parking area on the left. It is located near the end of the road.

Hiking directions: The High Road begins at the end of Paradise Road at the locked gate. The road skirts along the contours of the mountain, gaining a quick 200 feet up switchbacks before leveling off on a plateau. At 2 miles are the first views of Gibraltar Reservoir. The trail descends for a half mile, passing the Devil's Canyon Trail, to the junction with the River Trail. The right fork leads uphill to the top of the dam and Angostura Pass Road (Hike 56). The left fork leads to a swimming pool at the river and begins the return trip. The trail meanders down the canyon, frequently crossing the river back to the trailhead.

If you are here to cool off in a pool, take the River Trail (at the east end of the parking area) 0.3 miles to the popular Red Rocks pool. Just before the pool is a trail split. The left fork is the main trail to Gibraltar Dam. The right fork leads down to the shoreline. Red rock cliffs tower over the pool.

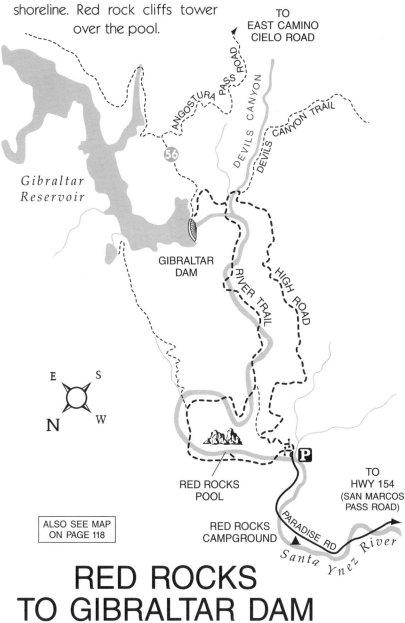

TO
EAST CAMINO
CIELO ROAD

ANGOSTURA PASS ROAD

DEVILS CANYON

DEVILS CANYON TRAIL

56

Gibraltar Reservoir

GIBRALTAR
DAM

RIVER TRAIL

HIGH ROAD

E S
N W

RED ROCKS
POOL

ALSO SEE MAP
ON PAGE 118

RED ROCKS
CAMPGROUND

TO
HWY 154
(SAN MARCOS
PASS ROAD)

PARADISE RD

Santa Ynez River

RED ROCKS
TO GIBRALTAR DAM

Hike 68
Tequepis Canyon

Hiking distance: 2 miles round trip
Hiking time: 1 hour
Elevation gain: 500 feet
Maps: U.S.G.S. Lake Cachuma
              The Cachuma Lake Recreation Area map

Summary of hike: The Tequepis Canyon hike follows the first section of the Tequepis Trail, which leads out of the canyon to West Camino Cielo Road, gaining 2,300 feet in four miles. The trail is well defined yet not heavily used. This hike parallels Tequepis Creek up canyon for one mile through a shady oak and sycamore forest. The trail crosses the creek three times.

Driving directions: From Highway 101 in Santa Barbara, take the State Street/Highway 154 exit. Turn right on Highway 154 (San Marcos Pass Road), and drive 16.9 miles to the signed turnoff for Ranch Alegre and Camp Whittier on the left. Turn left and continue 1.3 miles to the road's end at the designated parking area on the right.

Hiking directions: From the parking area, follow the paved road past the Tequepis Trail sign and ranch gate. Continue past the swimming pool to the Tequepis Trailhead at a signed junction. The paved road curves to the right. Take the trail bearing left, past the camp cabins and across Tequepis Creek. The trail crosses the creek a second time at 0.4 miles. Boulder hop across and continue south, remaining close to Tequepis Creek. At 0.6 miles, the trail crosses to the east side of the creek for the final crossing. At one mile, the trail narrows and sharply turns left, leaving the creek and beginning the ascent out of the canyon. This is the turnaround spot.

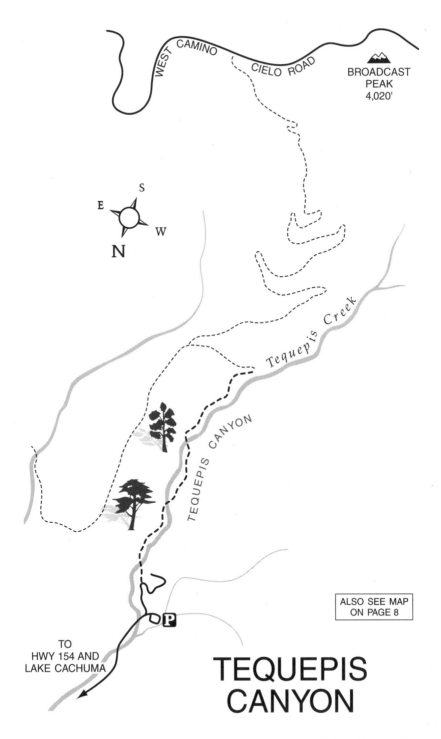

WEST CAMINO CIELO ROAD

BROADCAST
PEAK
4,020'

S
E W
N

Tequepis Creek

TEQUEPIS CANYON

ALSO SEE MAP
ON PAGE 8

P

TO
HWY 154 AND
LAKE CACHUMA

TEQUEPIS CANYON

Hike 69
Mohawk Mesa Trail
Lake Cachuma

Hiking distance: 0.6 mile loop
Hiking time: 15 minutes
Elevation gain: Level
Maps: U.S.G.S. Lake Cachuma
        The Cachuma Lake Recreation Area map

Summary of hike: The Mohawk Mesa Trail is a short, charming loop around a lakeside peninsula jutting into Lake Cachuma. The trail follows the perimeter of the land, circling around Mohawk Mesa. At the northern tip is Mohawk Point and a fishing pier.

Driving directions: From Highway 101 in Santa Barbara, take the State Street/Highway 154 exit. Turn right on Highway 154 (San Marcos Pass Road), and drive 17.5 miles to the Lake Cachuma County Park entrance on the right. Turn right and continue past the entrance kiosk, straight ahead for 0.1 mile. Turn right, following the signs to the overflow area. Continue 0.5 miles to the signed Mohawk Mesa Trail on the left. Park in the pullout by the trailhead.

Hiking directions: From the parking pullout, hike beside the northeast edge of Mohawk Mesa along Martini Cove. The forested path leads to Mohawk Point, overlooking Lake Cachuma on three sides. Near the northernmost point is a fishing pier. Along the way, several side paths lead down to the water's edge. The trail returns beside Drake Cove, a small, quiet inlet. Back at the park road, return to the trailhead on the left.

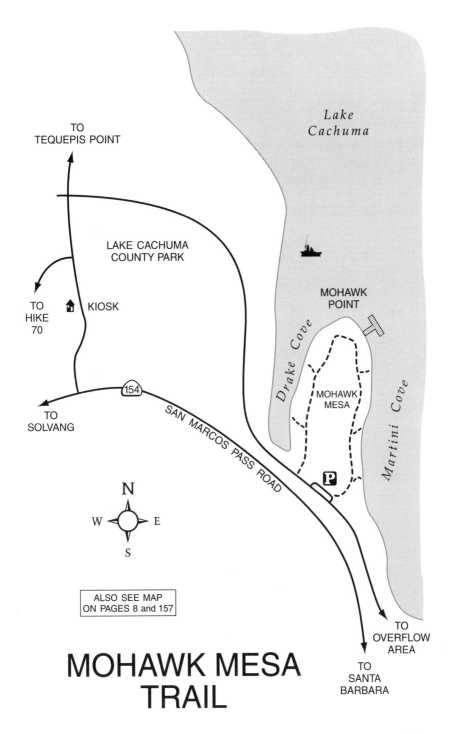

TO
TEQUEPIS POINT

*Lake
Cachuma*

LAKE CACHUMA
COUNTY PARK

MOHAWK
POINT

TO
HIKE
70

🏠 KIOSK

Drake Cove

MOHAWK
MESA

Martini Cove

154

TO
SOLVANG

SAN MARCOS PASS ROAD

Ⓟ

N
W ◀ ✦ ▶ E
S

ALSO SEE MAP
ON PAGES 8 and 157

MOHAWK MESA
TRAIL

TO
OVERFLOW
AREA

TO
SANTA
BARBARA

Hike 70
Sweetwater Trail to Vista Point
Lake Cachuma

Hiking distance: 5 miles round trip
Hiking time: 2.5 hours
Elevation gain: 160 feet
Maps: U.S.G.S. Lake Cachuma
   The Cachuma Lake Recreation Area map

Summary of hike: The 2.5-mile Sweetwater Trail begins at Harvey's Cove in Lake Cachuma. The cove is a beautiful inlet with a handicap-accessible fishing dock and picnic area under a grove of oak trees. The trail ends at Vista Point and Bradbury Dam, a scenic overlook near the west end of the lake. Along the way, the trail hugs the shoreline around inlets and coves, passing lake overlooks and meandering through an oak forest.

Driving directions: Follow the driving directions for Hike 69 to Lake Cachuma County Park. Turn into the park, and continue past the entrance kiosk. Take the road to the left for 0.3 miles to the trailhead parking lot at the road's end, following the signs to Harvey's Cove.

Hiking directions: From the parking lot, take the paved path around the south shoreline of Harvey's Cove. As you near the pier, take the hiking trail veering off to the left. The trail stays close to the water's edge, curving around each inlet. Once past Harvey's Cove, the trail curves inland and gains elevation, soon arriving at the Sweetwater Picnic Area. From the picnic area, follow the trail past the Vista Point sign, curving completely around Sweetwater Cove. At the south end of the cove, the trail joins an unpaved road for a short distance before picking up the trail again on the right and crossing a bridge. At 2.5 miles, the trail ends at the Vista Point parking lot and an overlook of the Bradbury Dam. Return along the same trail.

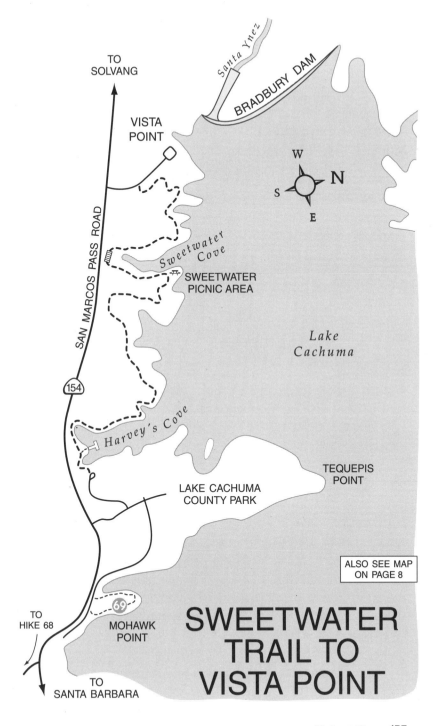

TO
SOLVANG

Santa Ynez

BRADBURY DAM

VISTA
POINT

W
S • N
E

Sweetwater
Cove

SWEETWATER
PICNIC AREA

SAN MARCOS PASS ROAD

154

Lake
Cachuma

Harvey's Cove

LAKE CACHUMA
COUNTY PARK

TEQUEPIS
POINT

ALSO SEE MAP
ON PAGE 8

TO
HIKE 68

69

MOHAWK
POINT

**SWEETWATER
TRAIL TO
VISTA POINT**

TO
SANTA BARBARA

Hike 71
El Capitan State Beach

Hiking distance: 1.5 miles round trip
Hiking time: 1 hour
Elevation gain: Level
Maps: U.S.G.S. Tajiguas
El Capitan and Refugio State Beach—Park Service Map

Summary of hike: El Capitan State Beach, located west of Santa Barbara, has a beautiful sandy beach with rocky tidepools. El Capitan Creek flows through a forested canyon to the tidepools at El Capitan Point. Nature trails weave through stands of sycamore and oak trees alongside the creek.

Driving directions: From Santa Barbara, drive 20 miles northbound on Highway 101 to the El Capitan State Beach exit. It is located 0.8 miles past the El Capitan Ranch Road exit. Turn left (south) and drive 0.3 miles to the state park entrance. Park in the day-use lot straight ahead.

Hiking directions: For a short walk, take the paved path down the hillside from the general store to the oceanfront. The quarter-mile paved trail follows the shoreline a short distance to the east before looping back to the parking lot.

For a longer hike, continue along the shore on the unpaved path past a picnic area to El Capitan Creek at the point. Near the mouth of the creek are the tidepools. Take the nature trail footpath, heading inland through the woods while following El Capitan Creek upstream. You will pass several intersecting trails that loop back to the park entrance station and parking lot. Near the entrance station, pick up the trail on the west side of the road. The trail parallels the western edge of El Capitan Creek through the forested canyon. The trail ends at a railroad bridge where the trail meets the road. Return by reversing your route or by exploring one of the intersecting nature trails.

To hike further, the Aniso Trail (Hike 72) continues along the shoreline to Refugio State Beach, 2.5 miles ahead.

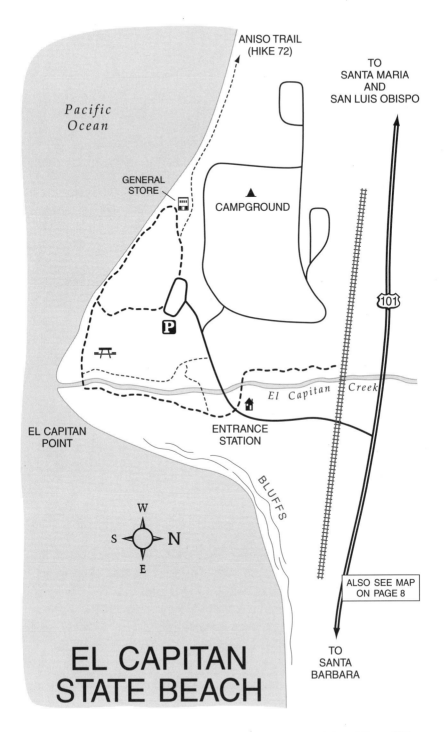

ANISO TRAIL
(HIKE 72)

TO
SANTA MARIA
AND
SAN LUIS OBISPO

Pacific Ocean

GENERAL
STORE

CAMPGROUND

101

P

EL CAPITAN
POINT

El Capitan Creek

ENTRANCE
STATION

BLUFFS

W
S — N
E

ALSO SEE MAP
ON PAGE 8

TO
SANTA
BARBARA

EL CAPITAN
STATE BEACH

Hike 72
Aniso Trail
El Capitan State Beach to Refugio State Beach

Hiking distance: 5 miles round trip
Hiking time: 2.5 hours
Elevation gain: Near level
Maps: U.S.G.S. Tajiguas

Summary of hike: The Aniso Trail (Chumash for seagull) is a paved hiking and biking trail along the sea cliffs and marine terraces connecting El Capitan State Beach to Refugio State Beach. The trail, an ancient Chumash trade route, follows the bluffs past weathered rock formations and secluded coves, offering constant views of the coastline. El Capitan State Beach sits at the mouth of El Capitan Creek in a extensive riparian woodland of coastal oaks and sycamores. Refugio State Beach, at the mouth of Refugio Canyon, has a palm-lined sandy beach cove and rocky shoreline with tidepools. Refugio Creek meanders through the park.

Driving directions: From Santa Barbara, drive 20 miles northbound on Highway 101 to the El Capitan State Beach exit. It is located 0.8 miles past the El Capitan Ranch Road exit. Turn left (south) and drive 0.3 miles to the state park entrance. Park in the day-use lot straight ahead.

Hiking directions: The paved trail begins on the north (right) side of the general store. Head west, skirting around the edge of the campground, and follow the contours of the cliffs past a lifeguard station. Two side paths descend to the beach and marine terraces. Descend from the bluffs to the beach at the south end of Corral Canyon. A side path curves left to Corral Beach, a small pocket beach. Continue straight ahead, returning to the bluffs past weathered rock formations. At 2.5 miles, the trail enters Refugio State Park near the palm-lined bay (back cover photo). Refugio Creek forms a tropical-looking freshwater lagoon near the ocean. Refugio Point, a low bluff, extends seaward at the west end of the beach. After exploring the park, return the way you came.

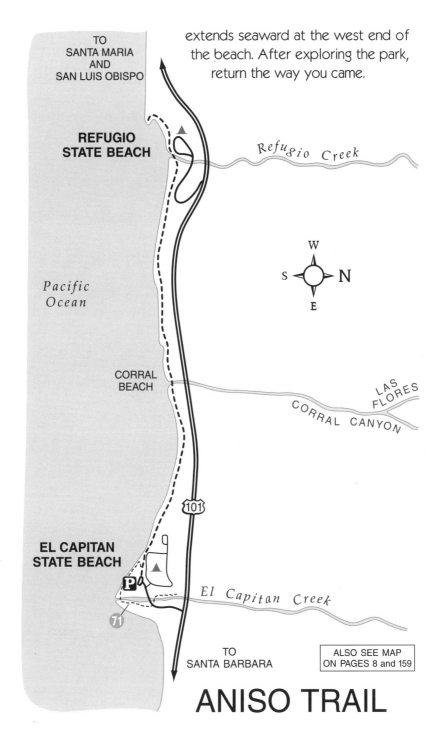

TO
SANTA MARIA
AND
SAN LUIS OBISPO

REFUGIO
STATE BEACH

Refugio Creek

W
N
S
E

*Pacific
Ocean*

CORRAL
BEACH

LAS
FLORES

CORRAL CANYON

101

EL CAPITAN
STATE BEACH

P

71

El Capitan Creek

TO
SANTA BARBARA

ALSO SEE MAP
ON PAGES 8 and 159

ANISO TRAIL

Hike 73
Beach to Backcountry Trail
GAVIOTA STATE PARK

Hiking distance: 3 miles round trip
Hiking time: 1.5 hours
Elevation gain: 750 feet
Maps: U.S.G.S. Gaviota
Gaviota State Park map

Summary of hike: In the mountainous backcountry of the 2,775-acre Gaviota State Park, a network of trails lead to scenic overlooks, sandstone outcroppings, intriguing caves and oak-studded rolling hills. This hike follows the Beach To Backcountry Trail across the rolling terrain to a vista point high above Gaviota Pass. There are great views of Gaviota Peak, the Pacific Ocean and the Channel Islands.

Driving directions: From Santa Barbara, drive 33 miles northbound on Highway 101 to the Gaviota State Park turnoff on the left. Turn left and drive 0.4 miles, bearing right near the entrance kiosk. Drive to the trailhead parking area on the right.

Hiking directions: Head north past the locked gate on the paved road. The half-mile road leads through dense scrub brush. A hundred yards before the end of the road is a signed multi-purpose trail on the left—the Beach to Backcountry Trail. Take this footpath up the south-facing hillside of the canyon. On the way up, views open to the Pacific Ocean and Gaviota Peak (Hike 76). The trail steadily zigzags up to a ridge. At one mile the trail levels out near large, sculpted sandstone outcroppings and caves. Begin a second ascent to the largest formation, and curve around to the backside of the outcropping. Cross a ravine and continue uphill to the top and a junction with the Overlook Fire Road. The left fork heads north along Hollister Ridge into the mountainous interior of Gaviota State Park. Take the right fork for a half mile, contouring up and down the rolling ridge. The panoramic overlook is located by the radio tower at the edge of the ridge where it drops off sharply on all three sides. After enjoying the views, return by retracing your steps.

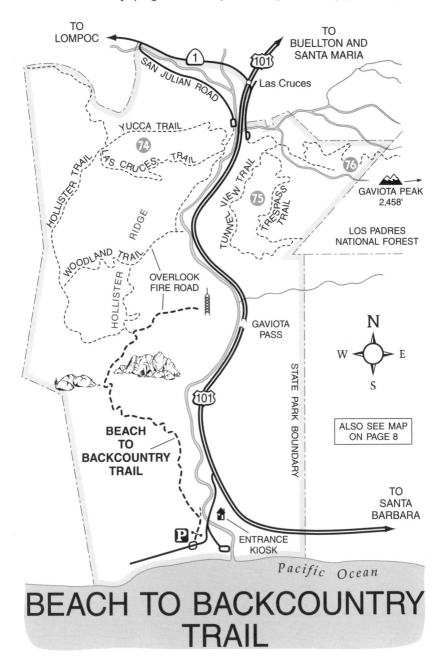

BEACH TO BACKCOUNTRY TRAIL

Hike 74
Yucca—Las Cruces Loop Trail
GAVIOTA STATE PARK

Hiking distance: 2 mile loop
Hiking time: 1 hour
Elevation gain: 600 feet
Maps: U.S.G.S. Solvang and Gaviota
　　　　 Gaviota State Park map

Summary of hike: This loop hike is part of a network of trails in the mountainous backcountry of the 2,775-acre Gaviota State Park. The Las Cruces Trail is an old ranch road crossing coastal grasslands and chaparral to Hollister Ridge, overlooking rolling hills and canyons. The Yucca Trail has phenomenal views of Gaviota Peak, the Pacific Ocean, the Channel Islands and the folded hills of the inland valley.

Driving directions: From Santa Barbara, drive 35 miles northbound on Highway 101 to the Highway 1/Lompoc exit. Turn left and drive 0.7 miles west to San Julian Road. Turn left and continue 0.8 miles to the gated trailhead at the end of the road. Park along the side of the road.

Hiking directions: Walk past the trailhead gate on the unpaved road along the west side of Highway 101. Pass large oak trees to a signed trail on the right at 0.2 miles. Begin the loop to the right on the Yucca Trail, winding up the hillside. Soon the gradient steepens and parallels the ridge leading up to the mountain top. Along the way, the Las Cruces Trail, the return route, can be seen to the south in the drainage below. Descend a short distance down the back side of the mountain to a T-junction with the Las Cruces Trail, an unpaved road on Hollister Ridge. Bear left and descend down the oak-studded canyon. Complete the loop and return to the trailhead.

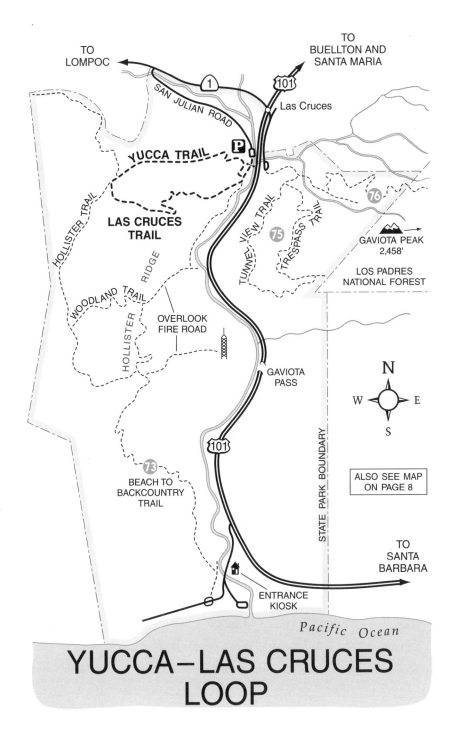

TO
LOMPOC

TO
BUELLTON AND
SANTA MARIA

SAN JULIAN ROAD

1

101

Las Cruces

P

YUCCA TRAIL

HOLLISTER TRAIL

**LAS CRUCES
TRAIL**

RIDGE

TUNNEL VIEW TRAIL

TRESPASS TRAIL

75

76

GAVIOTA PEAK
2,458'

LOS PADRES
NATIONAL FOREST

WOODLAND TRAIL

HOLLISTER

OVERLOOK
FIRE ROAD

GAVIOTA
PASS

N

W   E

S

101

73

BEACH TO
BACKCOUNTRY
TRAIL

STATE PARK BOUNDARY

ALSO SEE MAP
ON PAGE 8

TO
SANTA
BARBARA

ENTRANCE
KIOSK

Pacific Ocean

YUCCA–LAS CRUCES LOOP

Hike 75
Tunnel View—Trespass Trail Loop
GAVIOTA STATE PARK

Hiking distance: 2.5 mile loop
Hiking time: 1.5 hours
Elevation gain: 600 feet
Maps: U.S.G.S. Solvang and Gaviota
Gaviota State Park map

Summary of hike: This hike follows a forested path in Gaviota State Park at the base of Gaviota Peak. Along the way are shady groves of large, gnarled oaks and sycamores and open grasslands. There are panoramic views of the tunnels along Highway 101, the Pacific Ocean and the rolling hills of the inland valley.

Driving directions: From Santa Barbara, drive 35 miles northbound on Highway 101 to the Highway 1/Lompoc exit. Turn sharply to the right onto the frontage road, and continue 0.3 miles to the Gaviota State Park parking lot at the road's end.

Hiking directions: Head east past the trailhead sign on the wide, unpaved road under the shade of oak and sycamore trees. At 0.2 miles is a signed junction. The left fork leads to Gaviota Peak (Hike 76). Bear right on the Trespass Trail past large oak trees to a signed junction. Leave the old road and begin the loop to the right on the Tunnel View Trail. Cross over two seasonal drainages, and traverse the lower grassy foothills of Gaviota Peak. Cross Corral Springs on a lush stream-fed knoll. Curve east, heading up the hillside through a grove of stately oaks. At 0.7 miles, the path reaches an overlook on the ridge descending from Gaviota Peak. From the ridge are views of the Highway 101 tunnels and the Pacific Ocean. Bear left around the hillside up the stream-fed side canyon. Pass sedimentary rock outcroppings to a ridge at a T-junction with the Trespass Trail, the old ranch road. The right fork climbs steeply to Gaviota Peak. Bear left and descend on the wide path through chaparral and grass meadows, completing the loop. Take the right fork and return along the same trail.

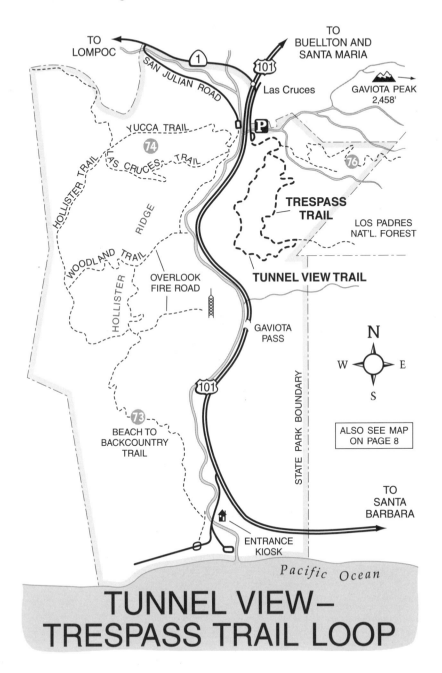

TUNNEL VIEW–
TRESPASS TRAIL LOOP

Hike 76
Gaviota Peak

Hiking distance: 6 miles round trip
Hiking time: 3 hours
Elevation gain: 1,900 feet
Maps: U.S.G.S. Solvang and Gaviota
Gaviota State Park map

Summary of hike: The trail to Gaviota Peak begins in Gaviota State Park near sea level and ends in the Los Padres National Forest nearly 2,000 feet higher. The trail passes Gaviota Hot Springs, a series of lukewarm, primitive sulphur spring pools that are popular for soaking. The hike to the peak is a substantial workout, but the views of the Santa Ynez Mountains, Las Cruces hills, Lompoc Valley, the Gaviota coastline and the Channel Islands are spectacular.

Driving directions: From Santa Barbara, drive 35 miles northbound on Highway 101 to the Highway 1/Lompoc exit. Turn sharply to the right onto the frontage road, and continue 0.3 miles to the Gaviota State Park parking lot at the road's end.

Hiking directions: Hike east past the trailhead on the wide, unpaved road under the shade of oak and sycamore trees. Stay on the main trail past a junction with the Trespass Trail (Hike 75). Cross a stream to a junction at 0.4 miles. The right fork is a short side trip to Gaviota Hot Springs. After enjoying the springs, return to the junction and continue on the left fork, following the old road as it curves around the grassy hillside. From here, there are views of the rolling hills and ranches of the Lompoc Valley. Long, gradual switchbacks lead up to the national forest boundary at 1.5 miles. At two miles, the trail reaches a saddle with more great views. The grade of the trail is never steep, but it rarely levels out. Near the top, pass a metal gate to a junction. The left fork follows the ridge east. The path straight ahead descends into San Onofre Canyon. Take the right fork for the final ascent to Gaviota Peak and the spectacular views.

Return along the same trail.

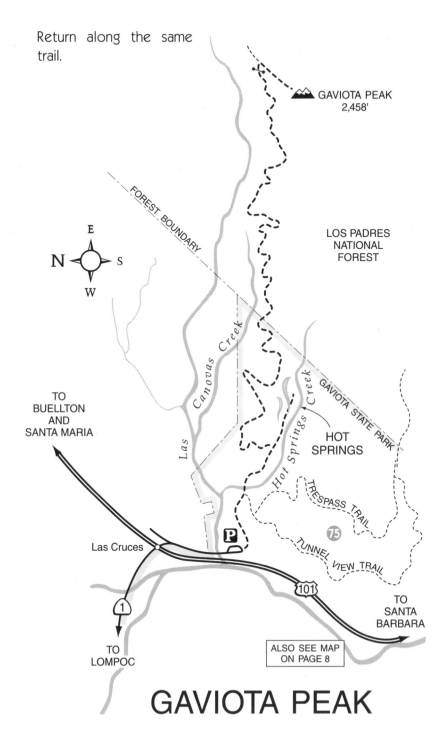

GAVIOTA PEAK
2,458'

FOREST BOUNDARY

LOS PADRES
NATIONAL
FOREST

N E S W

Las Canovas Creek

Hot Springs Creek

GAVIOTA STATE PARK

HOT
SPRINGS

TRESPASS TRAIL

75

TUNNEL VIEW TRAIL

TO
BUELLTON
AND
SANTA MARIA

Las Cruces

P

1

101

TO
LOMPOC

TO
SANTA
BARBARA

ALSO SEE MAP
ON PAGE 8

GAVIOTA PEAK

Hike 77
Nojoqui Falls

Hiking distance: 0.6 miles round trip
Hiking time: 30 minutes
Elevation gain: 50 feet
Maps: U.S.G.S. Solvang

Summary of hike: Nojoqui Falls is located in a cool, north-facing canyon in the grassy Nojoqui Falls County Park. The waterfall cascades 80 feet down a mossy, fern covered rock wall and into a pool. The well-maintained trail to the falls winds through a shady glen under oaks, bays, laurels and sycamores. The trail crosses three wooden bridges over a year-round creek on the way to the pool and grotto at the base of the falls.

Driving directions: From Santa Barbara, drive 38 miles northbound on Highway 101. Turn right at the Nojoqui Falls Park sign on the Old Coast Highway, 3.6 miles past the Highway 1 exit. Drive one mile to Alisal Road. Turn left and continue 0.8 miles to the Nojoqui Falls Park entrance on the right. Turn right and drive straight ahead to the last parking lot. If full, park in the first parking area.

Heading south on Highway 101, the Nojoqui Falls Park turnoff is 4.1 miles south of the Santa Rosa Road exit, the southernmost exit of Buellton.

Hiking directions: Hike to the trailhead at the south end of the second parking area. The wide path parallels Nojoqui Creek as it cascades down the narrow canyon. A series of three bridge crossings lead to the base of the falls below the sandstone cliffs. Relax on the large rock slabs and benches at the trail's end while viewing the falls.

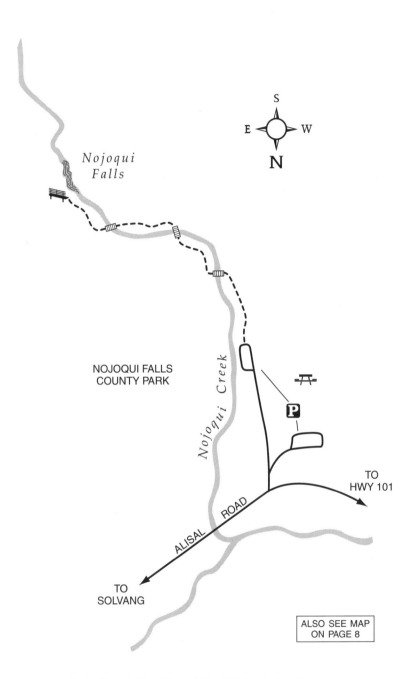

Nojoqui
Falls

NOJOQUI FALLS
COUNTY PARK

Nojoqui Creek

P

TO
HWY 101

ALISAL ROAD

TO
SOLVANG

S
E — W
N

ALSO SEE MAP
ON PAGE 8

NOJOQUI FALLS

Hike 78
Jalama Beach County Park

Hiking distance: 2 miles round trip
Hiking time: 1 hour
Elevation gain: Level
Maps: U.S.G.S. Lompoc Hills and Tranquillon Mountain

Summary of hike: Jalama Beach County Park is a picturesque 28-acre park at the mouth of Jalama Creek between Point Arguello and Point Conception. The park includes a year-round campground with a half mile of shoreline, a small wetland habitat, a picnic area and general store. This isolated stretch of coastline at the west end of the Santa Ynez Mountains is backed by cliffs and lush, rolling hills. For centuries it was a Chumash Indian settlement. It is now bordered by Vandenberg Air Force Base.

Driving directions: From Santa Barbara, drive 35 miles northbound on Highway 101 to the Highway 1/Lompoc exit. Turn left and drive 13.5 miles to Jalama Road. Turn left and continue 14 miles to the oceanfront campground and parking lot. A parking fee is required.

From Highway 101 in Buellton, take the Highway 246/Lompoc exit. Drive 16.2 miles west to Highway 1 in Lompoc. Turn left and continue 4.2 miles to Jalama Road. Turn right and continue 14 miles to the campground and parking lot.

Hiking directions: Follow the shoreline north for a short distance to the park boundary at Jalama Creek. The 30-foot bluffs above the creek are fenced. At low tide you may beachcomb northwest for a mile beyond the creek to the Vandenberg Air Force Base boundary. Along the way, cross narrow, rocky beaches with sheer cliff walls. Heading south, the sandy beach narrows and ends along the seawall cliffs. At low tide, the shoreline can be followed along the rock formations to a view of the lighthouse at Point Conception.

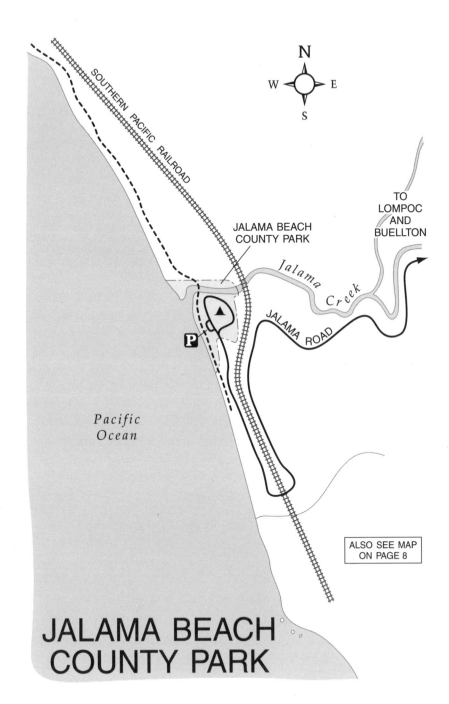

SOUTHERN PACIFIC RAILROAD

N

W ◆ E

S

TO
LOMPOC
AND
BUELLTON

JALAMA BEACH
COUNTY PARK

Jalama

Creek

▲

P

JALAMA ROAD

*Pacific
Ocean*

ALSO SEE MAP
ON PAGE 8

JALAMA BEACH
COUNTY PARK

Hike 79
El Camino Real—Sendero De Solis—
Las Zanjas Loop
LA PURISIMA MISSION STATE HISTORIC PARK
Open daily from 9 a.m.—5 p.m.

Hiking distance: 5 mile loop
Hiking time: 2.5 hours
Elevation gain: 300 feet
Maps: U.S.G.S. Lompoc
La Purisima Mission State Historic Park map

Summary of hike: The historic La Purisima Mission is one of California's 21 original Franciscan missions. Ten of the adobe buildings, dating back to the 1820s, are fully restored and furnished. The natural setting lies within the Lompoc Valley. More than 900 preserved acres surround the mission and create a buffer from development. The area has twelve miles of maintained trails that wind through the stream-fed canyon and cross the dunes and rolling terrain of the Purisima Hills. From the 480-foot summit are 360-degree vistas of Lompoc, Vandenberg and the rolling landscape.

Driving directions: From Highway 101 in Buellton, take the Highway 246/Lompoc exit. Drive 13.5 miles west on Highway 246 to Purisima Road. Turn right and continue 0.9 miles to the posted state park entrance. Turn right and park in the lot 0.1 mile ahead. An entrance fee is required.

Hiking directions: From the far (north) end of the parking lot, pass the visitor center and bookstore in the historic adobe buildings. Continue straight ahead past the mission buildings on the left. Walk past the picnic area in an oak grove to a gravel road and junction. Begin the loop to the left on El Camino Real, the original mission trail. Cross over Los Berros Creek towards the adobe blacksmith shop, passing Chumash Indian huts on the left. Stay on the main trail in Los Berros Canyon. Pass the Huerta Mateos Trail on the left, which climbs 100 feet up the dunes and through chaparral to a mesa and a network of trails. El Camino Real follows the west edge of the flat-bottomed canyon through open grasslands to the gated north boundary. Curve right along the boundary, crossing over Los Berros Creek, to a junction by ponderosa pines. The right fork, the Las Zanjas Trail, is the return route. For now, continue straight on Sendero De Solis, an unpaved maintenance road. Climb one mile up the hill on an easy grade to the water tanks at the summit. A path circles the two fenced tanks to magnificent vistas. Return to the junction in Los Berros Canyon, and take the Las Zanjas Trail to the left. Return along the east edge of the meadow. Follow the rock-lined water channel on the left, the mission's original aqueduct and irrigation system. Pass an old cistern and circular spring house, once used to collect water from the springs. Complete the loop and return to the visitor center.

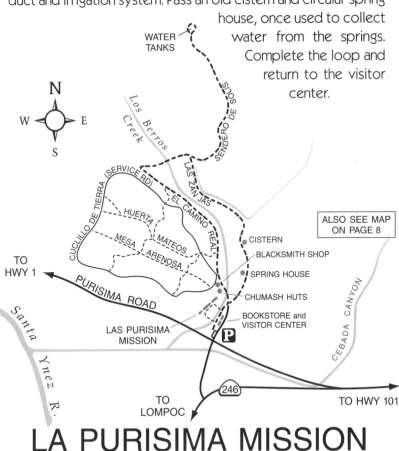

LA PURISIMA MISSION

Hike 80
Ocean Beach County Park

Hiking distance: 7 miles round trip
Hiking time: 3 hours
Elevation gain: Level
Maps: U.S.G.S. Surf

Summary of hike: Ocean Beach is a 36-acre park between Purisima Point and Point Arguello. The park borders the Santa Ynez River by a 400-acre lagoon and marsh at the mouth of the river. It is a resting and foraging habitat for migrating birds and waterfowl. Vandenberg Air Force Base, which surrounds the park, allows beach access for 1.5 miles north and 3.5 miles south.

Driving directions: From Santa Barbara, drive 35 miles northbound on Highway 101 to the Highway 1/Lompoc exit. Turn left and drive 17.7 miles to the Highway 246/Ocean Avenue junction in Lompoc. Turn left and continue 9.5 miles to Ocean Park Road. Turn right and go one mile to the parking lot at the end of the road by the Santa Ynez River.

From Highway 101 in Buellton, take the Highway 246/Lompoc exit. Drive 25.7 miles west, passing through Lompoc, to Ocean Park Road. (Highway 246 becomes Ocean Avenue in Lompoc.) Turn right and go one mile to the parking lot at the end of the road.

Hiking directions: To the north, a path borders the lagoon with interpretive nature panels. After enjoying the estuary, take the quarter-mile paved path along the south bank of the Santa Ynez River. Cross under the railroad trestle to the wide sandy beach. (Or take the footpath over the hill and cross the tracks.) Walk past the dunes to the shoreline where the river empties into the Pacific. At times, a sandbar separates the ocean from the river, allowing access up the coast. This hike heads south along the coastline. At just over a half mile, the railroad tracks curve away from the water as the dunes grow higher, rising 120 feet. The wide beach narrows to a strip at one mile.

Vandenberg Air Force Base sits atop the cliffs. At just over 3 miles, pass the mouth of Bear Valley, an extensive wetland. The beach soon ends as the cliffs meet the reef. Point Pedernales can be seen ahead,

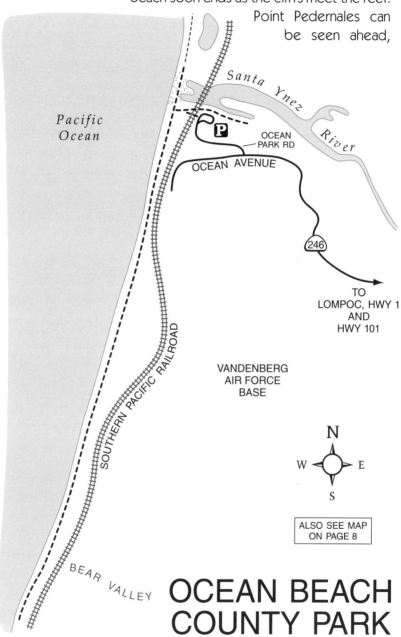

Pacific Ocean

Santa Ynez River

P

OCEAN PARK RD

OCEAN AVENUE

246

TO LOMPOC, HWY 1 AND HWY 101

SOUTHERN PACIFIC RAILROAD

VANDENBERG AIR FORCE BASE

N
W · E
S

ALSO SEE MAP ON PAGE 8

BEAR VALLEY

OCEAN BEACH COUNTY PARK

Hike 81
Point Sal Overlook

Hiking distance: 4 miles round trip
Hiking time: 2 hours
Elevation gain: 600 feet
Maps: U.S.G.S. Point Sal and Guadalupe

Summary of hike: This hike follows an old road through the rolling Casmalia Hills to several panoramic overlooks. The road, which crosses into Vandenberg Air Force Base, is open only to foot and bike traffic due to unstable soil and washouts. The spectacular views include Point Sal Ridge to Point Sal, the secluded Point Sal Beach at the base of the bluffs, Lion Rock, Point Arguello to the south, and to the north, Point Buchon at Montaña de Oro State Park.

Driving directions: From Highway 101 in Santa Maria, take the Betteravia exit, and head 7.7 miles west to Brown Road. Turn left and continue 5.1 miles to the signed junction with the Point Sal Road on the right. Turn right and park by the road gate.

Hiking directions: Walk past the locked gate, and follow the road uphill along the west edge of Corralitos Canyon. At 0.3 miles, the paved road turns to dirt, reaching a horseshoe bend at a half mile. Leave Corralitos Canyon and head south, reaching the first ocean overlook at one mile. Continue gently uphill, crossing Point Sal Ridge to a cattle guard at a fenceline. The road enters Vandenberg Air Force Base and becomes paved again. A short distance ahead is an abandoned air force missile tracking station on the left. The cinder block building has a wide stairway up to the concrete roof. From this overlook are commanding views up and down the scalloped coastline. Return to the road, and descend a few hundred yards to another overlook. The views extend along Point Sal Ridge to Point Sal. This is our turnaround spot.

To hike further, the road continues another 3 miles, descending 1,200 feet to the ocean. At the road fork, bear right. Near the shore, scramble down to the remote beach at Point Sal Beach State Park.

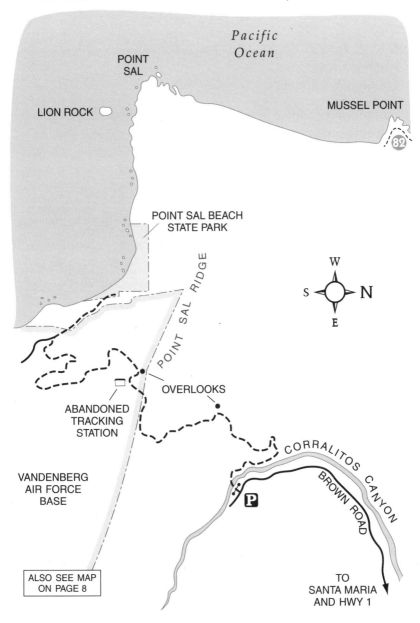

POINT SAL OVERLOOK

Hike 82
Guadalupe—Nipomo Dunes Preserve to Mussel Rock

Hiking distance: 6 miles round trip
Hiking time: 3 hours
Elevation gain: Level
Maps: U.S.G.S. Point Sal

Summary of hike: The Guadalupe—Nipomo Dunes Preserve sits among a range of towering, rolling sand mountains. This hike follows the isolated shoreline along the sandy beach, parallel to the highest sand dunes on the west coast. The north end of the preserve is bordered by the Santa Maria River and the county line. At the mouth of the river is a wetland area, providing a habitat for migrating shorebirds and native waterfowl. The south end of the dune complex is bordered by Mussel Rock, a towering 450-foot promontory jutting out into the sea.

Driving directions: From Highway 101 in Santa Maria, take the Main Street/Highway 166 exit, and head west towards Guadalupe. Drive 11.7 miles, passing Guadalupe, to the Guadalupe—Nipomo Dunes Preserve entrance. Continue 2 miles to the parking area on the oceanfront.

Hiking directions: Walk to the shoreline. First head north a half mile to the mouth of the Santa Maria River. The river widens out, forming a lagoon at the base of scrub covered dunes. At low tide, a sandbar separates the river estuary from the ocean, allowing easy access from the north along the Nipomo Dunes. Return to the south, meandering along the beach. Various side paths lead inland and up into the dunes. Follow the coastline towards the immense dunes at Mussel Rock. At 3 miles, reach the cliffs of Mussel Rock at the foot of the dunes. The enormous, jagged formation extends out into the ocean. For great coastal views to Point Sal, head a short distance up Mussel Rock to a sandy path that contours around to the south side of the formation. Return back along the beach to the parking area.

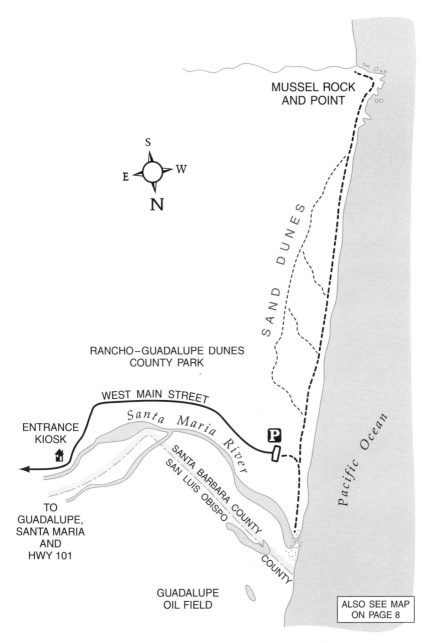

MUSSEL ROCK
AND POINT

S

E ⊕ W

N

SAND DUNES

RANCHO–GUADALUPE DUNES
COUNTY PARK

WEST MAIN STREET

Santa Maria River

ENTRANCE
KIOSK

P

Pacific Ocean

SANTA BARBARA COUNTY
SAN LUIS OBISPO
COUNTY

TO
GUADALUPE,
SANTA MARIA
AND
HWY 101

GUADALUPE
OIL FIELD

ALSO SEE MAP
ON PAGE 8

GUADALUPE–NIPOMO
DUNES PRESERVE

Other Day Hike Guidebooks

These books may be purchased at your local bookstore or
outdoor shop. Or, order them direct from the distributor:

The Globe Pequot Press
246 Goose Lane · P.O. Box 480 · Guilford, CT 06437-0480
www.globe-pequot.com

800-243-0495

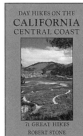

DAY HIKES ON THE
CALIFORNIA
CENTRAL COAST

71 GREAT HIKES
ROBERT STONE

DAY HIKES AROUND
MONTEREY
& CARMEL

77 GREAT HIKES
ROBERT STONE

DAY HIKES AROUND
BIG SUR

80 GREAT HIKES
ROBERT STONE

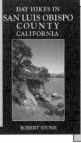

DAY HIKES IN
SAN LUIS OBISPO
COUNTY
CALIFORNIA

ROBERT STONE

DAY HIKES AROUND
SANTA
BARBARA

82 GREAT HIKES
ROBERT STONE

DAY HIKES IN
YOSEMITE
NATIONAL PARK

55 GREAT HIKES
ROBERT STONE

DAY HIKES IN
SEQUOIA
AND
KINGS CANYON
NATIONAL PARKS

ROBERT STONE

DAY HIKES AROUND
VENTURA
COUNTY

82 GREAT HIKES
ROBERT STONE

DAY HIKES AROUND
LOS ANGELES

83 GREAT HIKES
ROBERT STONE

DAY HIKES AROUND
LAKE
TAHOE

ROBERT STONE

DAY HIKES IN
YELLOWSTONE
NATIONAL PARK

54 GREAT HIKES
ROBERT STONE

DAY HIKES IN
GRAND TETON
NATIONAL PARK
AND
JACKSON HOLE

ROBERT STONE

DAY HIKES IN THE
BEARTOOTH
MOUNTAINS

RED LODGE, MONTANA TO
YELLOWSTONE NATIONAL PARK
ROBERT STONE

DAY HIKES AROUND
BOZEMAN
MONTANA

INCLUDING THE GALLATIN
CANYON AND PARADISE VALLEY
ROBERT STONE

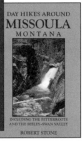

DAY HIKES AROUND
MISSOULA
MONTANA

INCLUDING THE BITTERROOTS
AND THE SEELEY-SWAN VALLEY
ROBERT STONE

DAY HIKES ON
OAHU

57 GREAT HIKES
ROBERT STONE

DAY HIKES ON
MAUI

55 GREAT HIKES
ROBERT STONE

DAY HIKES ON
KAUAI

55 GREAT HIKES
ROBERT STONE

DAY TRIPS ON
ST. MARTIN

ROBERT STONE

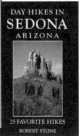

DAY HIKES IN
SEDONA
ARIZONA

25 FAVORITE HIKES
ROBERT STONE

Notes

About the Author

For more than a decade, veteran hiker Robert Stone has been writer, photographer and publisher of Day Hike Books. Robert resides summers in the Rocky Mountains of Montana and winters on the California Central Coast. This year-round temperate climate enables him to hike throughout the year. When not hiking, Robert is researching, writing and mapping the hikes before returning to the trails. Robert has hiked every trail in the Day Hike Book series. With over twenty hiking guides in the series, he has hiked over a thousand trails throughout the western United States and Hawaii.